Dutch
Oven
Secrets

Dutch Oven Secrets

Lynn Hopkins

Cover art by Fred VanDyke

ISBN: 0-88290-372-1
Horizon Publishers' Catalog and Order Number: 1214

Printed and distributed
in the United States of America by

Horizon
Publishers
& Distributors, Incorporated
P.O. Box 490 Bountiful, Utah 84011-0490

Contents

Chapter 1

Introduction

The second time I ever cooked in a Dutch oven was in the World Championship Dutch Oven Cook-off. I had heard advertisements on the radio and thought it sounded fun. I called one of the committee members and after a short pep talk, I was signed up for two nights to cook. During my conversation with the committee member, she mentioned cooking with charcoal briquettes. What a novel idea! It sounded easy enough.

The day of the competition came. I gathered my few tools and an old bag of charcoal my wife's grandmother had given us, and headed for the competition. I had planned to make a vegetable medley. I had plenty of time so I meticulously cut up all the vegetables and arranged them in a large bowl to look pretty. Then I waited. I tried walking around to other contestants to help relieve some of my anxiety, but it only seemed to increase it. Finally it was time to start the briquettes.

I dumped out a pile of briquettes, just as I had seen others do, poured on some lighter fluid and lit the match to them. They burst into flames. As the lighter fluid burned out so did the fire and my briquettes still weren't lit. To remedy the situation, I poured more fluid on the briquettes. The flames lasted a little longer but the briquettes still didn't light. How embarrassing! I was entered in a world championship cook-off and I couldn't even get my fire lit. I tried and tried, but to no avail. I had gone through a 12-inch stack of newspaper and a full can of lighter fluid. Those briquettes were not going to light!

With only fifteen or twenty minutes until I was to be judged, a dear couple in the pit next to mine recognized my plight and offered the use of their coals. The vegetables had a slight "bone" to them, but they were warm.

I learned two very important lessons that day. First, you can't beat the type of people that cook in Dutch ovens. They are the greatest. If you make a Dutch oven cook your friend, you have a friend for life. Some people say it is the food that keeps people cooking in the big black pots, others say it is the friendships. I say it is both. The second thing I learned was to never use 10-year-old charcoal—especially in a contest.

I'm not claiming to be the world's greatest Dutch oven cook. All I want to do with this book is share a few secrets I have learned over the years to help make Dutch oven cooking as enjoyable for you as it has been for me. This book will take you from buying a new Dutch oven to cooking for a crowd. You may not be interesed in all the chapters, but hopefully, you can find a few secrets to adapt to your own style of cooking. Whatever your goal, bon appetite.

Chapter 2

Dutch Oven Care and Handling

I remember how excited I was when I acquired my first Dutch oven. I was anxious to get into the wilds and cook with it, but I had no idea how to start. I searched the box the oven came in and found a little slip of paper that told how to season my Dutch oven. I studied it and did exactly what it said. I didn't want to ruin my oven without even being able to cook in it once! Since then I have learned that Dutch ovens are very forgiving and take a lot of abuse. I also learned that there are a lot of ways to "season" a Dutch oven. I heard of people filling the oven with salt and oil and baking it. Others just cooked up a good batch of extra-greasy potatoes and called their oven seasoned. Some people use all-vegetable oil and others use animal fats. I mention this to let you know there is more than one way to season a Dutch oven. The method suggested in this chapter is the one I prefer. If you have an aluminum Dutch oven refer to the section on Aluminum Dutch oven care later in this chapter.

First, let's concentrate on what to do with the oven when you get it. This process is called "seasoning" your Dutch oven. Generally, it is only done once, unless your oven becomes rusty or something happens to the seasoned finish and you need to start over. Follow these simple steps and you'll be successful every time.

Seasoning a Cast-iron Dutch Oven

1. Remove the oven from the box. Make sure the lid is there and everything is intact and free of cracks and chips. If your oven is cracked or broken, return it for exchange or refund.

2. Wash the oven in warm soapy water. When the oven leaves the factory it is sprayed with a clear sealant to keep it from rusting while in storage. This sealant must be removed before trying to season the oven. Look for any rust. If there is any, remove it with steel wool or a small wire brush. It is very important to start the seasoning process with a clean, rust-free oven.

3. Dry your oven thoroughly and place it on a heat source. A heat source could be a hot fire, a gas barbecue grill or in a 350° too 400° oven. Regardless of the heat source, *never allow the oven to become heated to the point of being cherry red.* This causes the oven to warp or even break. The lid will never seat properly again, which will limit what can be cooked in the oven. Most people do not like seasoning their Dutch oven in the kitchen because it tends to smoke up the house.

Seasoning a Cast-iron Dutch Oven.

4. When the oven is hot (approximately 350° to 400°) remove it from the heat source and wipe on a *very thin* coat of all-vegetable oil, coating the entire oven and lid inside and out.

5. Return the oven to the heat source until it stops smoking.

6. Remove the oven and wipe on another *very thin* coat of all-vegetable oil and then let it cool.

7. The oven is now considered "seasoned." If a Dutch oven is well-seasoned and cleaned properly after each use, it will turn jet black with the beautiful shiny surface typical of a well-cared-for Dutch oven.

Cleaning a Cast-iron Dutch Oven

There are many ways to clean a Dutch oven. I have seen people turn ovens upside down on the fire and burn them out. Another method is to wash them out after each use. I don't care for either method. They both destroy the "seasoning" you worked so hard to establish, making it necessary to re-season the oven after each use. That's a lot of extra work, and if you re-season after each use you are missing out on some of the best-tasting food you can make. After you have used a Dutch oven for a period of time and have built up the "seasoning," you get tastes out of your oven otherwise not possible. Personally, this is why Dutch oven cooking is so distinctive and everyone says that everything tastes better when cooked in a Dutch oven.

Here's how to clean your Dutch oven without having to re-season it:

1. Remove all food from the oven. Wipe it as clean as you can. Use a putty knife to remove any food that is stuck to the oven.

2. If the oven will not wipe clean, add approximately one cup of warm water and swirl it around with a rag or washcloth until the sugar or food dissolves. If water is scarce at the campsite, dampen a washcloth and wipe the inside until the oven is clean. Empty any excess water from the oven, then dry it thoroughly. If the food is especially stubborn in coming out of the oven, salt can be used as a scouring agent. If

salt is used, be sure to clean out the oven well so your next meal won't taste salty.

3. Place the oven on a heat source. A heat source could be a hot fire or a 350° to 400° oven. Regardless of the heat source, *never allow the oven to become heated to the point of being cherry red.* This causes the oven to warp or even break. The lid will never seat properly again, which will limit what can be cooked in the oven.

4. When the oven is hot (approximately 350° to 400°); remove it from the heat source and wipe on a very thin coat of all-vegetable oil, coating the entire oven inside and out. When cool, your Dutch oven is now ready for storage.

Storing Cast-iron Dutch Ovens

Last winter, I left all my Dutch ovens out on the back porch for quite a while. When I did bring them into the basement, I didn't notice that my son had put a little bit of water in each oven. They just got placed downstairs to wait for spring. You can imagine how I felt when I opened the ovens and discovered every one of them was rusted. I can't blame my son because I should have checked them before putting them in the basement.

Storing a Dutch oven with a paper towel in the lid to help with the air circulation.

The most important thing to remember when storing a Dutch oven is that water and moist air can be fatal. Try to store your ovens in dry places where the air circulates freely. Avoid places where it will get cold and you could have a problem with condensation. Store your ovens with the lid ajar so air can circulate inside the oven to dry out any condensation. A paper or cloth towel can be placed inside the oven to absorb any excess moisture. Another good idea is to check them occasionally during the storage period to make sure there is no condensation that can cause rust building up.

When you remove your oven from storage, check for dust accumulation and any rust. Wipe the dust away, remove any rust and re-season. If there is not any rust you don't need to re-season the oven, just wipe it out with a cloth that has a little oil on it. You are now ready for another season of great cooking.

Starting Up a Cast-aluminum Dutch Oven

The care of cast-aluminum Dutch ovens is very different than that of cast-iron Dutch ovens. Remove the oven from the box. Wash thoroughly with warm soapy water. Let dry. You are now ready to cook. The aluminum Dutch oven does not need to be seasoned at any time.

Cleaning a Cast-aluminum Dutch Oven

Remove all food and wash in warm soapy water. Aluminum Dutch ovens can also be washed with steel wool, cleansers, sand, or in the dishwasher. Over time, the inside will remain shiny bright and the outside will become dark colored. This is the desired appearance of an aluminum Dutch oven. The dark coloring aids in heat absorption.

Storing a Cast-aluminum Dutch Oven

Because you are not concerned with destroying your seasoning coat in an aluminum Dutch oven, you can store your oven anywhere and anyway you like. Just be sure the oven is cleaned well before you use it again.

Chapter 3

Tools and Cooking Accessories

Cooking in a Dutch oven does not require any special tools other than something to lift the lid from the pot and lift the oven from the fire. The only tools I had when I started were a pair of pliers and a "mit" hot pan holder. But there are tools and accessories which make the process easier and more enjoyable. This chapter describes the typical items which serve to simplify the Dutch oven cooking process. They are not listed in any specific order of importance or usefulness.

1. Oil

Although oil is not directly counted as a tool, it is necessary to keep your cast-iron Dutch oven functional. The oil is what gives the oven its non-stick protective coating. This coating helps prevent rust formation. All-vegetable oil is preferred over animal fats. Animal fats can leave a salty taste in the oven and are more prone to rancidity.

2. Paper Towels, Rags or Burlap

Wiping materials may not be readily accepted as tools, but they are very basic in their function. It is important to clean the oven after use so mold and rust will not form on the inside of the oven. Both these conditions, rust and mold, can pit and deteriorate the surface of the oven, making it harder to clean and shorter lived. Rags, towels or burlap are used to clean the oven and are also very useful in applying thin coats of oil in the seasoning and cleaning process. (Cleaning and seasoning of the oven were covered in detail in chapter 2 on Dutch oven care and handling.)

3. Long- or Short-handled Ax

Unless you have a ready supply of wood, a long- or short-handled ax is a necessity. Large logs need to be split to be burned faster and small limbs need to be cut into manageable lengths for the fire.

4. Long- and/or Short-handled Dutch Oven Tools

"Dutch oven tools" can make Dutch oven cooking a lot easier. The term "Dutch oven tools" refers to implements used to lift the oven out of the fire and to lift the lid from the oven. The long-handled tool can reduce back strain by making it unnecessary to bend over to lift the lid or pot from the fire. The long-handled tool, when used in conjunction with the short one, can be used to dump the contents from the oven. Either tool can be used to stir or rearrange coals or charcoal during the cooking process.

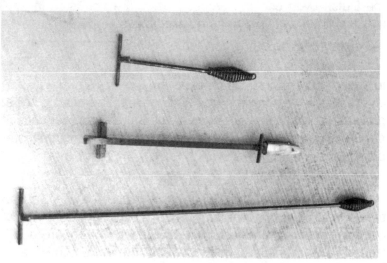

Long- and short-handled Dutch oven lifters and lid lifters.

5. Shovel and/or Long-handled Tongs

When cooking with Dutch ovens, you need some way of moving coals or charcoal to where they will be most beneficial. A short-handled Army shovel works well to move coals when you use coals from a wood fire. The shovel can be folded into a smaller size to help facilitate easier packing and storage. It also enables you to pick up quite a few coals at a time and can also be used to stir the fire. Soil can be moved to level the cooking site with the shovel. If cooking in a deep pit or burying your oven, a shovel is an obvious necessity. A fire can be put out with a shovel by throwing shovelfuls of dirt to smother the flames. The list can go on and on if your imagination is used, but the important point to remember is that the shovel is a very useful tool.

Long-handled tongs can be used as a partial substitute for a shovel. Obviously tongs cannot be used to dig a pit or move soil, but they can be used to move coals and charcoal to where they will be most beneficial. They seem to work better with charcoal than with wood fire coals because of the size of particles in each instance. Wood coals are many different sizes ranging from the size of a small pea to the size of a log. Large coals are easy to move around with tongs but the small coals are almost impossible to move.

Charcoal briquettes burn evenly so they are all relatively the same size. Charcoal briquettes are large enough that they are easily handled with tongs. Handling coals and charcoal with tongs can be time consuming. Generally you can only pick one coal or briquette up at a time. However, even though it takes extra time, tongs work better than a shovel when working with briquettes. Briquettes are almost round in shape so it is hard to get them onto the shovel, and once they are on the shovel, it's hard to make them stay on it.

6. A Thick Leather Glove, Hot Pads or Mit

Many times when you're using your oven, the fire gets very hot. When you're seasoning or cleaning your oven, the oil may pop or splash and burn you. These burns, although generally not serious, can be painful and annoying. A thick leather glove,

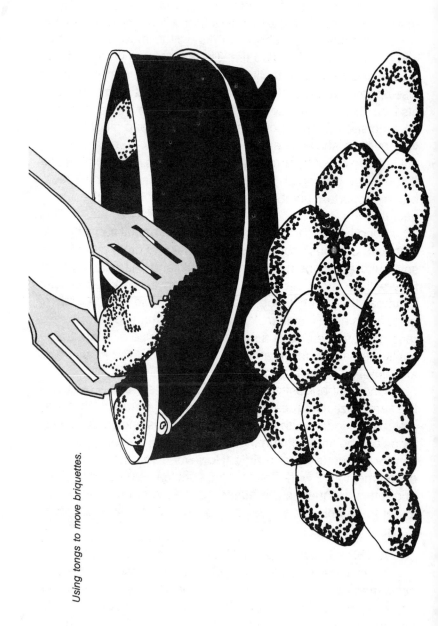

Using tongs to move briquettes.

hot pad or mit can be used to help prevent this discomfort. However, all safety precautions should be observed, even when using these helpful tools. Don't try to remove the oven from the fire using only the glove or mit. And don't try to hold a hot pan with only a glove or mit on. These tools can be very useful, but don't overestimate their insulating capabilities.

7. Cooking Table

A cooking table can be very useful while preparing your favorite Dutch oven meals. A table raises your work surface so you aren't having to bend over for long periods. Tables can relieve a lot of back pain and trouble. There are portable models

Dutch oven cooking table with other accessories.

available which enable you to transport them anywhere you wish to go. Once you have used one, you won't want to be without one ever again.

8. Long-handled Spatula, Spoon, Fork and Tongs

When cooking over a hot fire these utensils can help you manage your food and still stay away from the heat. They are more a convenience tool than anything.

9. Charcoal Lighter or Lighter Fluid

Charcoal lighters come in many shapes and sizes. They can be made from five gallon cans. Cut a hole in the side and mount a grate halfway down the side of the can. The charcoal is placed in the top and crumbled newspaper is placed through the hole in the side of the can. The papers are lit and then replenished when burned until the briquettes are burning well. Commercially produced units can be purchased.

Many people may not cook with charcoal enough to justify buying a briquette starter so they just use common lighter fluid. Either way, both are useful to insure a ready supply of hot "ready-to-go" coals.

10. Small, Narrow Putty Knife

A flexible putty knife is a very useful tool when cleaning the inside of a Dutch oven. Use it to scrape baked-on residue from the inside of the oven. A putty knife will greatly decrease the clean-up time of a Dutch oven.

11. Whisk Broom

A whisk broom is very useful for removing coals and ashes from the Dutch oven lid. If coals are removed before the lid is removed it's less likely that ashes will fall from the lid into the food. There also is less problem with wind blowing ashes into other ovens that may be open.

12. 3 Large Nails or Railroad Spikes

The first year I was in the Cook-off, I baked a carrot pineapple cake. I didn't even think to have my oven level so obviously, it wasn't. My cake was one inch thick on one side and three inches thick on the other. When I realized what I had done it was too late to redistribute the batter so I moved the coals around so the cake wouldn't burn on one side and be raw on the other. I think I told the judges it was my leaning tower of Pisa carrot pineapple cake. This could have been avoided if I would have used large nails or railroad spikes to pound in the ground to create a level spot on the ground to cook on. When pounded into the ground in a triangle formation, they create a very sturdy working surface on which to set the oven or lid. Water can then be poured into the oven to check for complete levelness.

13. Lid Racks

In another cook-off, I made barbecued chicken and beef and pork ribs, all in the same pot. It was getting close to being done when I noticed the sauce was a little runny. I took the lid off the oven and, for lack of a better place to set it, I set the lid on the grass. That is when I learned how important lid racks can be. I killed the grass where the lid was setting and I got docked five points for not keeping my equipment sanitary. Since then I have found many suitable substitutes. Lid racks can be anything on which to set a lid to prevent it from getting dirty and killing the lawn. The nails mentioned above could be used or a small wooden frame. Metal racks can be used but are usually very heavy and bulky. I have even used large rocks when I was in a pinch and didn't have anything else. Just let your imagination go.

14. Dutch Oven Nylon Storage and Handling Bags

If you travel much with your Dutch oven, or if you just take them up to the canyon every now and then, nylon storage and handling bags are a must for you. No longer will everything in your trunk be black when you get where you're going from rubbing against the ovens during the trip. They will be neatly tucked away in their own individual bags to keep them from getting or causing everything else in the trunk to get dirty. Even if you don't travel with them, these bags are great to store the ovens in. They are less likely to get rusty and dirty, thus saving you valuable time every spring cleaning them up.

Dutch oven cooking bags

As you can see, there are many tools that can help make Dutch oven cooking easier. Though all of them are not necessary, they combine to make the cooking experience more pleasant. When looking at the list you may wonder how you can most easily get all the tools to your campsite, or move them from one place to another. A camp chuck wagon or cook box can be used. These tend to be large and bulky. However, they do provide storage capacity for both food stuffs and tools alike. These boxes can range from the size of a briefcase up to as large as a pick-up truck bed. Grub boxes also are very handy in providing means to secure food and equipment from predators and vandalism.

If a cook box doesn't suit your needs, nylon bags can be purchased to store your tools and equipment in. These bags may seem appealing but as of yet they are not designed to carry much more than your actual Dutch oven tools. You may be able to squeeze a few other tools in, but not many.

Plastic storage boxes may be just what you need for storage and transportation if you don't have tools and utensils. These boxes can be purchased at most hardware stores and come in a variety of colors.

Consider having two sets of tools if you cook a lot with your oven. You could use one set while camping and the other while at home. Many tools are made at home by do-it-yourselfers. Your only limitation is your own imagination.

Chapter 4

Heat Sources

The last few morsels had just been cleaned from our plates and we had retired from the table to some more comfortable lawn chairs. The summer heat was made bearable only by the late afternoon shade of the house. Suddenly, we were jolted back to the real world by the screams of my eighteen-month-old son. Somehow he had slipped away from his cousins and gone out to the garden, where we had been cooking, to do some discovering. When we finally got to him, he was standing in the hot coal bed with his bare feet. Luckily for us, the coals were mostly burned out so he didn't get burned. But it still pointed out the most important point to be remembered concerning fires and heat sources — *safety!* Always think ahead and be ready for anything. Consider your surroundings and the climatic conditions. Dutch oven cooking can be fun and rewarding, but it's dangerous if you are not careful.

There are many sources of heat that will enable you to cook in a Dutch oven. These versatile pots have been used in kitchens on the stove, in the oven and on backyard gas grills. They have been seen in roaring bonfires and in deep pits. Charcoal, propane or even coal have all been used as heat sources.

For purposes of this book I will describe the two most popular heat sources: coals from wood fires and from charcoal. If you are interested in some of the other heat sources, there are some general guidelines at the end of this chapter.

Coals From Wood Fires

There are many ways to build a fire and everyone has his own way, so a complete description will not be written here. If you need a good reference on fire building, check the *Boy Scout Handbook.* Here are some points to remember about cooking with wood coals.

Cook with Coals, Not an Open Flame

Let the flame die down so you are only cooking with coals. I remember my first experience with Dutch oven cooking. My family had been hiking all day so we were very tired and hungry. When we got back, Dad built the fire for the Dutch oven chicken and Mom started a batch of bread for scones.

When Dad finally got a bunch of coals ready, he put the oven, chock full of chicken, into the hot coals to bake. Looking back now, I'm not sure if it was lack of patience or too few coals, but the chicken was not cooking fast enough for my dad. To rectify the situation, he threw a couple chunks of wood on top of the oven to help get some more heat. Ten or fifteen minutes later Dad took the oven from the fire to check its progress. As Dad lifted the lid, all our hearts sank as huge clouds of billowing black smoke came pouring out of the oven. When the smoke finally died down, we were only able to find a few ashes. All the chicken was gone.

Flames create more heat than coals, and heat from a flame is very irregular and hard to control.

Have a Large Supply of Coals Available

Build a large fire and have a lot of coals available to cook with. Wood coals do not seem to last as long as charcoal briquettes. For this reason, a lot of people like to use two pits when cooking. They cook in one pit and keep a fire going in the other for a constant supply of hot coals. There is nothing more frustrating than to have some food *almost* cooked and run out of heat from your coals or charcoal. This happened to me one time when I was cooking for a large church group. The food finally got done but the crowd was surely getting restless, and we all know how unpleasant for the cook a restless crowd can be. It's not hard to keep a few extra coals going, and it is well worth it if it means waiting an extra twenty minutes or more to eat while you get more coals to cook with.

Don't Forget Your Shovel

A shovel is an absolute must when working with wood coals. Use it to move coals around to where the heat is needed.

All Woods Are Not Created Equal

All woods do not burn at the same rate. Hard woods burn slower and hotter than soft woods. This does not mean that you should only use one type of wood, it just means that you need to be aware of some of the differences. Another difference in wood is between evergreen trees and deciduous trees. Evergreen trees have a resin or "pine gum" that can cause "hot spots" in your fire. Don't stop using evergreen wood, just remember to rotate your oven and lid more frequently. (This procedure is described at the end of this chapter under hints to control heat sources, #3).

Charcoal Briquettes

Dutch oven cooking went through a small revolution at the introduction of cooking with briquettes. Briquettes helped eliminate huge roaring bonfires and the cooks being distressed by smoke inhalation. The briquettes provide an easy way to manipulate heat evenly so it is where you want it. When briquettes were first made available, some of the old sourdoughs threw out their wood fires and have only used briquettes since. They definitely are an important convenience item in Dutch oven cooking. You can still build the fire and cook with wood coals, but charcoal is much easier to use.

There are many brands of charcoal available on the market. Some cooks swear by one brand and would not think of using another. Other cooks use a different brand and are just as satisfied. This may seem confusing to the beginner, but don't let it bother you. My advice is to try as many different varieties as you can, then decide which *you* like best. Price and availability should have a lot to do with your choice.

Regardless of the brand, never cook with briquettes indoors. Even though they don't give off very much smoke, they give off a toxic gas that can be fatal. You won't have any problem with this toxic gas when cooking out-of-doors because of the open ventilation.

A pile of burning charcoal briquettes.

Charcoal briquettes give off a lot of heat for their size. To heat a 12-inch Dutch oven to 350°F, it only takes 8-10 briquettes under the oven and 10-13 on the lid. Charcoal briquettes burn evenly so you are not as susceptible to have hot spots. Briquettes are easy to move to exactly where the heat is needed with a pair of long-handled tongs. Briquettes can be lit in the traditional manner with charcoal lighter fluid and matches or you can use a handy charcoal lighter that uses old papers for fuel. These lighters are also very handy to keep some briquettes going so hot coals will be available to replenish the burned-out briquettes.

I have found that after briquettes burn a while, they build up a layer of ash which acts like an insulating coat, keeping all the heat inside. All you have to do to release the heat is tap them every now and again to knock off the ash layer. Listed at the end of this chapter is a chart to show how to determine the temperature of your fire. This method will work both for briquettes and for wood coals.

Hints to Help Control Heat Sources

1. If you take the lid off your oven and the contents are boiling so heavily you cannot see the food, your fire is too hot. Remove a few coals.

2. If you take the lid off and the contents are not boiling after being on the fire for twenty minutes, your fire is too cold. Add more coals.

3. If half your meat, rolls, cobbler, etc. is browning faster than the other, you have a hot spot. Rotate the oven one-quarter turn to the left and rotate the lid one-quarter turn to the right every 5 to 10 minutes until the dish is cooked.

4. HEAT RISES! Some foods such as chicken and potatoes can be cooked with only bottom heat. Cakes, breads, and anything "baked" needs to have bottom *and* top heat. In the case of baked foods, remember to put more heat on the lid of your oven than under it. This helps force the heat down and cook the food more evenly.

5. Anytime you cook with wood coals, rotate the oven one-quarter turn to the left and the lid one-quarter turn to the right, every 5 to 10 minutes. Wood coals are often a variety of sizes so rotating the oven helps eliminate "hot spots."

6. When cooking under windy conditions, be aware that the wind "fans" one side of the coals, causing them to burn faster and hotter on one side. Set up a wind break and be sure to rotate the oven as described above.

7. When baking in a cast-iron Dutch oven, place most of the coals on the lid around the outside edge. The cast-iron conducts heat very well so you will get uniform browning. If you place too many coals in the middle of the lid you could get hot spots.

8. Cast-aluminum Dutch ovens heat up and cool down fast. They require a closer watch on food so you do not get

scorched foods. The cast-iron ovens are more forgiving. They are slower to heat up, slower to cool and the heat is more evenly distributed. Food cooked in a cast-iron Dutch oven does not need to be checked as frequently as food cooked in a cast-aluminum Dutch oven. I mention the cooking qualities of these ovens in this chapter only to help you understand how closely you need to watch your heat source to guard against hot spots.

How to Determine Fire Temperatures
Hand Method

This method is the most convenient to use. Just hold your hand about three inches over the spot on which you will be cooking. The length of time you are able to hold your hand there will determine the heat of the fire.

The heat and temperature table listed on this page corresponds with the length of time you are able to hold your hand over the fire.

Counts*	Heat	Temperature		
6 to 8	Slow	120°	-	175°C
		250°	-	350°F
4 to 5	Moderate	175°	-	200°C
		350°	-	400°F
2 to 3	Hot	200°	-	230°C
		400°	-	450°F
1 or less	Very Hot	230°	-	260°C
		450°	-	500°F

*1 count=1 second

The hand method of determining fire temperatures.

Chapter 5

The Three Basic Dutch Oven Cooking Techniques

Almost all Dutch oven cooking requires the use of one of three basic techniques: (1) bottom-heat cooking, (2) baking, which is combined bottom-heat and top-heat cooking, and (3) slow pit cooking. These techniques can be combined or used individually to provide the type of heat desired. This chapter will explain the three basic techniques and point out their applications along with their strengths and limitations.

Bottom-heat Cooking

With bottom-heat cooking, the Dutch oven is being used like a frying pan, usually with the lid off. In this book I often refer to it as "basic cooking." Top heat can be added to decrease cooking time, but it is not necessary. The recipes in this book are referring to bottom-heat cooking if they say "cook" or "use bottom heat only," or when they tell you to "brown" or "saute" something. With this type of recipe your Dutch oven can be used indoors on your stove top, utilizing only the heat from a stove-top heating element.

Bottom-heat cooking, or basic cooking, is the easiest method of using your Dutch oven. However, the menus you will be able to cook will be limited. Therefore, I will introduce you to the second technique: of baking.

Baking (Combined Bottom-heat and Top-heat Cooking)

Baking in a Dutch oven is almost the same as basic cooking. The difference is made when you add coals to the lid of the oven instead of only having bottom heat.

Baking will enable you to make cobblers, pies, cakes, rolls and breads, and a host of other yummy treats. As mentioned earlier in "hints to help control heat sources," the most important thing to remember is that heat rises! You will need more coals on the lid of your oven to help push the heat down to the food. If you have more coals on the bottom, your food will burn every time. If there aren't enough coals on the lid the food will cook very slowly — if at all. It will also be very hard to brown anything you are baking.

To help explain the basics of Dutch oven baking, I'll briefly describe the process of baking cakes, bread and pies.

Cakes. Mix together a cake mix or a cake from scratch as the directions indicate. Pour the batter into a greased 12-inch Dutch oven. *Making sure the oven is level,* place the oven over 8 briquettes and place 14 briquettes on the lids. A tilted oven will cause one side of the cake to bake faster than the other side. To prevent hot spots, rotate the oven and also the lid one quarter turn every 5 to 10 minutes. Be careful — don't jar the oven or your cake may fall. Check the cake after 15-20 minutes to make sure it isn't cooking too fast.

When done, the cake will spring back when touched. Let the cake rest for a few minutes, then turn it out on the lid. If you prefer not to turn the cake out on the lid, take the cake off the heat source before it is completely cooked. Cast-iron Dutch ovens retain heat and will continue to cook the cake after the oven is removed from the coals. Be careful or you'll burn it. Frost when cool and enjoy.

Breads. Bread and rolls are cooked very similarly to cakes. However, it isn't as essential to have the oven as perfectly level when cooking them as it is with cakes.

Place the bread or rolls in the oven. Put the lid on and place on a heat source that is the temperature called for in the recipe. Remember to rotate both the oven and lid every 5 to 10 minutes so you will get even cooking and browning.

Pies. Baking pies in a Dutch oven takes a little practice to master the technique. The hardest part is to get the crust into the oven without it breaking apart. This can be accomplished by rolling the dough out 1/8 of an inch thick on top of plastic wrap. Now you can lift the dough up and handle it easily because it clings to the plastic wrap. Place the dough in a cool oven and press it into place, using the plastic wrap to keep the dough from sticking to your hands. Using a knife, cut away the excess dough that will not be needed and flute the edges.

To bake a single crust place the oven over 8 briquettes for 4 minutes. Move the oven immediately from the bottom heat and place 40 coals on the lid and cook until the shell is well browned.

If you are baking a double crusted pie place the filling in the bottom shell, then roll out the top crust as you did the bottom one. Place on the pie and trim with a knife or kitchen scissors. Seal together with the bottom crust and flute the edges. Bake as you would a cake or rolls at the temperature indicated in the recipe.

If using a cast-iron Dutch oven don't let your crust get too dark before removing the oven from the fire. The pie will continue to brown after it has been taken from the fire because the iron retains the heat.

For your convenience, these same hints and tips are found in each of the chapters for cakes, breads and pies.

Slow Pit Cooking

Often when people hear the phrase, Dutch oven cooking, they envision the cook digging a hole, building a fire in it, throwing the oven in, then burying the whole deal. This method works well if you are going to be gone all day and want a real nice meal ready when you get back. It works just like a crock pot. However, I wouldn't recommend cooking anything this way that needs frequent checking. It would be easy to wear a good cook out trying to dig up and rebury the oven each time it needed to be checked.

This is the slow pit method I have found to work well for me.

1. Dig a hole 6 inches wider than your Dutch oven and 2 to 2½ feet deep. Example: For a ten-inch Dutch oven, dig a hole 16 inches wide and 2 to 2½ feet deep.

2. Build a large fire *in the hole* and keep it burning for about one hour. Building the fire in the hole dries the soil out so it will be a better insulator to keep the heat around the Dutch oven after it has been covered up. Throw 7 or 8 good sized rocks in the fire after the fire has been burning 15 to 20 minutes. These rocks will heat up and retain the heat along with the coals.

3. Prepare the ingredients and place them in the Dutch oven.

4. With the lid securely in place, set the oven in the hole on top of the coals. Move the coals and rocks around so there are some on all sides and on top of the oven. But at all times when the oven is in the pit MAKE SURE THE DUTCH OVEN IS LEVEL.

5. Fill the hole in with dirt. Some people like to put a piece of tin over the oven before burying it to help insure the oven from getting dirt in it when uncovered.

6. Go have a wonderful day!

7. 6 to 8 hours later, dig up the Dutch oven being very careful as you are digging not to pry off the lid and knock dirt into your food. Remove the oven from the pit and sweep or dust the dirt off the oven.

8. Eat and enjoy!

Most people when cooking with this method do not rely on a written recipe. Many people just throw a roast and vegetables in the oven and that is good enough. I suggest you try a few crock pot recipes and then add your own variations. A little practice and experimentation could reap great benefits.

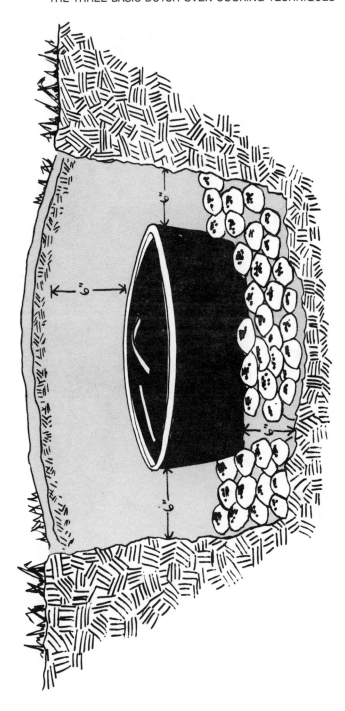

Artist's drawing of slow pit cooking.

Chapter 6

Vegetable Dishes

Dutch Oven Potatoes I

1 12-inch Dutch oven
½-1 lb. bacon
3 large onions, thinly sliced and separated into rings
5 lbs. potatoes, peeled and thinly sliced
salt and pepper to taste
1-2 cups grated Cheddar cheese

Cut bacon into 1-inch pieces. Place in Dutch oven and put on fire to "cook." Stir the bacon frequently to prevent scorching. When browned, use one-third of the potatoes to make a layer over the bacon pieces. Using one-third of the onions, make a layer over the potatoes. Salt and pepper to taste. Continue making layers until the oven is full, adding salt and pepper as you go. Do not over fill the oven or the lid will not seat properly and the food will take longer to cook. Place the lid on the oven and cook on a 350° fire, 8-10 briquettes under the oven. If the potatoes do not cook fast enough more coals can be added under the oven or you can combine the "basic" cooking method with the "baking" method and add 10 to 13 coals to the lid. Check the potatoes by stirring every 5 minutes. Test potatoes for doneness by piercing with a knife or fork. When potatoes are done, top with cheese. Replace the lid and return the oven to the fire until the cheese is bubbly. Serve immediately. This recipe will serve 12-15 hungry campers.

NOTE: If you are cooking these potatoes on a gas or electric range in your kitchen, leave the lid off the oven and stir more frequently.

Dutch Oven Potatoes II

4 pounds potatoes
1/2-1 pound bacon
4-5 carrots
3-4 medium-sized onions

Put in a Dutch oven and add a little water. Cook till almost done. Add:

1 can cream of mushroom soup
1 can Eagle Brand Sweetened Condensed Milk
1 can mushrooms

Cook until done, add cheese to the top and heat till melted. Makes 12-15 servings.

Potato Casserole

about 5 lbs. potatoes
1 8 oz. package cream cheese
1 can cream of mushroom or chicken soup
1 large container sour cream
2 cups grated cheese
1/2 small onion

In a 12-inch or smaller Dutch oven, saute onions in butter or margarine. Add the creamed soup, sour cream and creamed cheese. Cook over medium heat until smooth, stirring constantly to avoid scorching. In a 12-inch Dutch oven par boil the potatoes until tender all the way through. Peel the skins off and grate them into a large bowl. Pour the soup mixture over the potatoes. Stir in half of the grated cheese. Spoon into a 12-inch Dutch oven. Sprinkle remaining cheese on top. Bake over a 350° fire for 30 minutes or until warmed all the way through. Makes 12-15 servings.

New Peas and Potatoes

5 lbs. new red skinned potatoes
4 cups fresh peas (you can also use frozen)
1 cube butter or margarine
12 heaping tablespoons flour
8 cups milk
1 heaping tablespoon of each Thyme, Rosemary, and Tarragon
Salt and Pepper to taste

Scrub all of the potatoes. Leaving the skins on, cut into 1-inch pieces. Add enough water to cover. Add 1 Tablespoon salt. Boil until tender when pierced with a fork. Add the peas and cook 5 minutes more. Drain and set aside.

Melt the cube of butter in the Dutch oven. Add the spices and saute for a few minutes to release the flavor. Add the flour and mix well. Add the milk very slowly. If you add it too quickly the sauce will be lumpy. Stir constantly to avoid scorching. When the sauce has thickened, add the potatoes and peas. Makes 12-15 large servings.

Mollyanne's Baked Beans

1 lb. ground sausage
1 medium onion, chopped
2 cans pork and beans
¼ cup mustard
¾ cup catsup
½ cup brown sugar

Over a medium fire, brown the sausage. Saute the onion with the sausage. When the onions are clear, drain the grease from the sausage. Add the remaining ingredients and mix well. Bake on a moderate fire, (7-8 briquettes under the oven and 13-14 on the lid) for one hour. Makes 10-12 servings.

Swiss Cheese
and Mushroom Quiche

Crust

>   1 cup flour
>   ⅓ cup cold butter
>   3 tablespoons cold buttermilk

Cut together the flour and butter. Use a pastry cutter or two forks. If butter is unsalted, add ¼ teaspoon salt. Try to work quickly so ingredients stay cold. When the mixture is uniformly blended, add the buttermilk (or water, but buttermilk is worth it) or enough so that the mixture holds together enough to form a ball. Chill the dough at least one hour. Roll out dough and put in an 8-inch Dutch oven as described in the section on pies.

Quiche

>   1½ cups Swiss cheese, grated
>   1 medium onion, chopped
>   ¼ pound mushrooms, chopped
>   butter
>   salt
>   pepper
>   thyme
>   4 eggs
>   1½ cups milk
>   3 tablespoons flour
>   ¼ teaspoon salt
>   ¼ teaspoon dry mustard
>   paprika

Cover the crust with the cheese. Saute the onion and mushrooms in butter; sprinkle with salt, pepper, and thyme. Put this mixture on top of the cheese. Mix together eggs, milk, flour, ¼ teaspoon salt, and dry mustard; beat well. Pour this custard mixture over the mushroom layer. Sprinkle with paprika. Bake over a 400° fire until the center is solid when jiggled. Makes 8 servings.

Vegetables in Chicken Sauce with Dumplings

2 cups broccoli pieces
2 cups cauliflower pieces
2 cups whole small mushrooms
3 cups new small potatoes
3 cups new small carrots
1 cup small pearl onions
2 cans Campbell's cream of chicken soup
1 can Campbell's cream of mushroom soup
1 cup grated mild cheese
2 cups Bisquick
2/3 cup milk
1 cup water
1/4 cup butter
salt and pepper to taste

Clean and measure all vegetables, then put in a bowl and set aside. Heat Dutch oven and wipe clean with vegetable oil. Put 1 cup warm water and vegetables into Dutch oven, steam for 15 minutes. Add butter, cream of mushroom and cream of chicken soup. Mix well and bring to a boil. Add cheese and stir in.

Dumplings
Combine 2 cups Bisquick and 2/3 cup milk to form a soft dough. Make dumplings and drop into the boiling vegetables and sauce. Bake over a 350° fire (7-8 briquettes on the bottom and 11-13 briquettes on the lid) until golden brown. Makes 10 servings.

Garden Vegetable Combination with Butter Sauce
Peggy Roskelly and Rosemary Parkinson

Carrots
Broccoli
Mushrooms
Tomatoes
Cauliflower
Peas
Summer Crookneck Squash

Any combination of fresh vegetables can be used. Steam carrots, cauliflower, and broccoli until slightly done. Put squash in steamer for a few minutes. Arrange in a Dutch oven (the size will depend on how many vegetables) with ¼ cup water on the bottom. Steam until vegetables are done to taste. Very little heat, if any, should be on the bottom with about 10 briquettes on the top. The mushrooms can be sauteed on the Dutch oven lid. The tomatoes should be set on as a garnish, after all the other vegetables are cooked.

Butter Sauce
> ½ cup butter (softened)
> ¼ teaspoon salt
> 2 green onions chopped fine
> 4 tablespoons freshly grated parmesan cheese

Melt butter. Stir in remaining ingredients. Drizzle over the hot vegetables.

Chapter 7

Breads, Biscuits and Rolls

Breads

Breads and rolls are cooked very similarly to cakes. However, it isn't as essential to have the oven perfectly level as with cakes.

Place the bread or rolls in the oven. Put the lid on and place on a heat source that is the temperature called for in the recipe. Remember to rotate the oven and lid so you will get even cooking and browning.

Scrambled French Toast

4 eggs
3 tablespoons sugar
$1/_8$ teaspoon nutmeg
8 slices of bread cubed
6 tablespoons butter
1 cup milk
$1/_2$ teaspoon salt
$1/_2$ teaspoon cinnamon

Beat eggs, milk, sugar, and spices. Melt butter in a 12-inch Dutch oven or use an inverted lid over the fire. When hot, pour in the egg mixture and bread cubes. Cook with folding strokes until golden brown. Serve with your favorite syrup. Makes 4 servings.

Perfect White Bread

1 package active dry yeast
¼ cup warm water (110°)
2 cups milk
2 tablespoons sugar
1 tablespoon shortening
2 teaspoons salt
5¾-6¼ cups all purpose flour

Soften yeast in warm water. In Dutch oven, combine milk, sugar, shortening and salt. Heat until sugar dissolves. Cool to lukewarm. Stir in 2 cups of flour. Beat well. Add the softened yeast, beat thoroughly until smooth. Add enough remaining flour to make a moderately stiff dough. Turn out onto a lightly floured surface and knead till smooth and elastic (8-10 minutes). Shape into a ball. Place in lightly greased bowl, turn once to grease entire surface. Cover, let rise in a warm place until double (about 1¼ hours).

Punch down dough. Turn out on lightly floured surface. Divide dough into 2 portions. Shape each into a smooth ball, cover and let rise 10 minutes. Shape into loaves, place in a 12-inch Dutch oven. Cover and let rise in a warm place for 15 to 20 minutes. Bake over a 375° fire about 45 minutes or till done. Remove from the Dutch oven to cool. Makes 2 loaves. Can be mixed in a mixer.

Cheese Bread

Scald 1 cup milk. Remove from heat and add 3 tablespoons sugar, 1 tablespoon salt and 1 tablespoon soft butter or margarine. Set milk mixture aside to cool. Add to warm water and stir 2 tablespoons or 2 packages active dry yeast, and 1 cup warm water. Place in a large bowl 4½ cups flour, 1½ cups grated cheddar cheese. Add and mix well the yeast mixture and the milk mixture. Cover with a towel, let rise one hour. Spoon into a 10-inch Dutch oven. Bake over a 375° fire for 35 minutes. Makes 1 loaf.

French Bread

½ cup warm water
2 packages yeast
3 tablespoons sugar
⅓ cup oil
1 tablespoon salt
2 cups warm water
6 cups flour

Combine all ingredients with half of the flour. Mix well. Add the rest of the flour. Form into two loaves by rolling into 9″ × 12″ shape and roll dough like a jelly roll. Place in a greased 16-inch Dutch oven and let raise until double (30-60 minutes). Bake over a 400° fire for 30 minutes. Makes 2 loaves.

French Cheese Braid

1 package active dry yeast
¾ cup warm water
1 tablespoon sugar
1 teaspoon salt
3 eggs
½ cup margarine or butter, softened

3½ - 4 cups of flour
1½ cups swiss cheese, diced
vegetable oil
1 egg yolk
2 tablespoons water

Dissolve yeast in warm water in large bowl. Stir in sugar, salt, eggs, margarine and 2 cups of the flour. Beat until smooth. Stir in remaining flour to make the dough easy to handle. Turn dough onto a lightly floured surface and knead until smooth and elastic. Place in a greased bowl. Cover and let rise in a warm place until double. Punch down the dough and knead in the cheese until well distributed. Divide into three equal parts. Roll each part into a rope 15-inches long. Place ropes together in lightly greased 16-inch Dutch oven. Braid ropes together gently but loosely. Do not stretch. Pinch the ends to fasten and tuck under securely. Brush with oil. Let raise 20 minutes. Beat the egg yolk and 2 tablespoons water slightly. Brush over the braid. cover and place over a 350° degree fire, 25 to 30 minutes or until the braid sounds hollow when tapped. Makes one braid.

Bread Sticks

1 tablespoon instant dry yeast	1 tablespoon honey
1½ cups warm water	1 teaspoon salt
1 tablespoon malted milk powder	4 - 4½ cups flour

Combine yeast and warm water. Let stand until yeast is dissolved. Add malted milk powder, honey and salt. Mix to blend. Add the flour gradually until dough forms a ball.

Knead a few times on a lightly floured board. Divide the dough in half, set one-half aside.

Divide the remaining half into 12 pieces. Roll into sticks no thicker than ½ inch. Melt ½ cube of butter in the bottom of a 16-inch Dutch oven and dip the sticks in it. Sprinkle with parmesan, poppy seeds or seasoned salt. Bake over a 350° fire for 15-20 minutes or until the bread sticks are golden brown. Repeat the process for the other half of the dough. Makes 24 bread sticks.

Angel Biscuits

5 cups flour	1 tablespoon yeast
¾ cup shortening	½ cup warm water
3 teaspoons baking powder	2 cups buttermilk
1 teaspoon soda	3 tablespoons sugar
1 teaspoon salt	

Sift dry ingredients, cut in shortening. Dissolve yeast in warm water, stir into buttermilk. Add to flour mixture. Do not overmix. Cover and put in the fridge. Pat out the dough on a flat, lightly floured surface and cut into biscuits with a glass. Cook over a 400° fire for 12-15 minutes in a 12- or 14-inch Dutch oven. Makes about 18 biscuits.

Sky-High Biscuits

2 cups all-purpose flour
1 cup whole wheat flour
(or 3 cups all-purpose flour)
4½ teaspoons baking powder
2 tablespoons sugar

½ teaspoon salt
¾ teaspoon cream of tartar
¾ cup margarine or butter
1 egg, beaten
1 cup milk

In a bowl, combine the flours, baking powder, sugar, salt and cream of tartar. Cut in butter or margarine until the mixture resembles coarse cornmeal. Add egg and milk, stirring quickly and briefly. Knead lightly on floured surface. Roll or pat gently to 1″ thickness. cut into 1-2″ biscuits. Place in a 12- or 14-inch Dutch oven. Bake over a 450° fire for 10-12 minutes. Makes about 12 biscuits.

Orange Rolls

1¼ cup milk (scalded)
½ cup margarine
½ cup sugar
1 teaspoon salt
2 cakes or 2 tablespoons yeast dissolved
   in ½ cup warm water
⅓ cup orange juice
2 beaten eggs
⅓ cup evaporated milk
5 - 6 cups flour (non-sifted)

Mix as usual for rolls. Let rise until double. Roll out ½″ thick and spread margarine on dough. It can now be made into rolls or fancy breads at this point by rolling and cutting cinnamon roll style, or cutting them out parker house style. Bake over a 375° fire for 15-20 minutes or until done. This dough may be frozen for about 2 weeks. Makes about 2 dozen rolls.

Pizza Dough

2 cups warm water
2 tablespoons dry yeast
1 teaspoon salt
4 tablespoons shortening
2 teaspoons sugar
7 cups flour

Mix warm water, shortening, yeast, salt and sugar in a large bowl. Let stand until yeast softens. Work in the flour gradually and knead until smooth. Cover and place in a warm spot until dough doubles in size. Divide in fourths. Let rest. Use two of the portions to make a crust for a 12-inch Dutch oven, three for a 14-inch Dutch oven and use all four portions to make a crust in a 16-inch Dutch oven. Place your favorite toppings on the crust and bake over a 450° fire for about 12 to 15 minutes or until the crust is browned. Makes two 12″, one 14″ or one 16″ pizza.

Balloon Buns

⅔ cup warm water
2 tablespoons yeast
½ cup shortening
4 cups hot water
6 cups flour

½ cup sugar
2 teaspoons salt
2 eggs
Large marshmallows
Melted butter
Cinnamon sugar

Dissolve the yeast in the ⅔ cup of warm water. Add the shortening to the hot water and let it sit until melted and cooled to lukewarm. Add the flour, sugar, and salt to the yeast mixture. Add the eggs and a little sugar if you like your bread sweeter. Add more flour until the dough is thick but moist. Turn the dough out onto a floured surface and knead until smooth and bubbly. Let rise until double; punch down and let rise again.

Break pieces off one at a time. Flatten dough. Roll a large marshmallow in melted butter and then cinnamon sugar mixture and put in the center of the dough piece. Fold dough around it and seal together. Put sealed side down in a greased 16-inch Dutch oven after dipping the top in melted butter. Let rise about 1 hour. Bake at 350° for 15-20 minutes or until golden brown. Makes about 24 Balloon Buns.

Chapter 8

Sourdough Recipes

Sourdough Starter

1 cup raw milk or buttermilk   1 cup flour

Mix well and let stand 48 hours or until it starts to ferment. Each time a start is used from your starter add 1 cup flour and 1 cup evaporated milk. If the starter is not used once a week, freeze to keep it from getting too active.

Sourdough Basic Batter

For any recipe which calls for basic batter, do as follows—
The evening before you want pancakes, waffles or breadstuffs, measure 1 cup of sourdough starter from your sourdough pot into a large mixing bowl. Use a large enough bowl to allow batter to ferment and rise (about 2 qts.). Do not use a metal bowl. Add 2 cups of lukewarm water and about 2½ cups of flour. Mix thoroughly. This mixture will be thick and somewhat lumpy but will thin down during the night of fermentation. Cover your bowl and set in a warm place. It is important to keep batter warm so it will ferment properly.

Thin Sourdough Pancakes

2 cups basic batter
2 tablespoons cooking oil
2 tablespoons sugar
1 teaspoon salt

1 egg
1 cup evaporated milk
1 teaspoon baking soda

Combine the basic batter, egg, cooking oil and milk and beat thoroughly. Combine salt, soda and sugar and blend together until smooth, eliminating any lumps of soda. Sprinkle evenly over the top of batter and fold in evenly. This will cause a gently forming, rising action. Allow batter to rest a few minutes and fry in a hot, lightly greased 16-inch Dutch oven or on the lid. Makes 12 4″ pancakes.

Thick Sourdough Pancakes

½ cup starter
1 cup warm water
1½ cups flour
1 teaspoon soda

1 cup undiluted evaporated milk
2 eggs
½ teaspoon salt
2 tablespoons sugar

Combine the starter, milk, water and flour in a large bowl. Mix to blend and leave at room temperature overnight. The next morning add eggs, sugar, salt and soda and mix well. (Do not beat.) Fry in a hot, lightly greased 16-inch Dutch oven or on the lid. Makes 12 4″ pancakes.

Sourdough Scones

2 cups sourdough starter
3 tablespoons sugar
1 teaspoon salt

3 tablespoons shortening
½ teaspoon soda
½ teaspoon baking powder

Mix and stir well the above ingredients. Add approximately 2½ to 3 cups flour. Break off with hands and pat flat. Fry in hot grease. Makes 12 or more scones.

Sourdough Biscuits

½ cup starter
2 cups flour
1 tablespoon sugar
1 teaspoon baking powder

½ teaspoon soda
1 cup milk
¾ teaspoon salt
bacon grease or butter

Mix the starter, milk and 1 cup of the flour in a large bowl. (Do this the night before if you are serving the biscuits for breakfast, or in the morning if you want them for dinner.) Cover the bowl and keep at room termperature to let raise.

Turn this very soft dough out onto ½ cup flour on a breadboard. Combine salt, sugar, baking powder and soda with remaining 1½ cups flour and sift over the top. With your hands, mix the dry ingredients into the soft dough. Knead lightly to get the right consistency. Roll out to a ½-inch thickness. Cut out each biscuit with a cutter and dip each in either warm bacon grease or melted butter. Place close together in a 10- or 12-inch Dutch oven and set them in a warm place to let rise for about 30 minutes. Bake over a 400° fire for 15-20 minutes or until golden brown. Makes 12 biscuits.

Sourdough Hot Rolls

To at least 1½ cups of the leftover thin pancake batter, stir in enough flour (plus ½ teaspoon salt for each cup of flour) to form a stiff dough. Turn out on a floured board and knead (adding flour as necessary until it is a smooth ball with a satiny finish). Place in a greased bowl, brush with melted butter, and allow to rise in a warm place for about 1 hour. Punch down, turn out on a floured board and knead again (adding more flour, if needed). Roll out to ¾-inch thickness. Cut with biscuit cutter. Dip each round on both sides in melted butter, and place just touching in a 12- or 14-inch Dutch oven. Let rise until nearly double (about one hour). Bake over a 400° fire for 15-20 minutes. Serve while still hot. Makes 12 or more rolls.

Sourdough Cornbread

1 cup sourdough starter	2 eggs, beaten
1½ cups evaporated milk	¼ cup melted butter, warm
1½ cups yellow corn meal	½ teaspoon salt
2 tablespoons sugar	½ teaspoon soda

Mix the starter, milk, corn meal, sugar and eggs together in a large bowl. Stir in melted butter, salt, and soda. Turn into a greased 10-inch Dutch oven and bake over a 450° fire for 25-30 minutes. Makes 8 servings.

Sourdough Half-and-Half Bread

6-12 hours before you make this bread, combine:
> 1 cup sourdough starter
> 1 cup milk
> 2 cups whole wheat flour

Beat vigorously, then allow to ripen in a warm spot.

1¾ cups milk	1 cup whole wheat flour
2 tablespoons butter	1 teaspoon salt
¼ cup honey	½ teaspoon baking soda
1 tablespoon active dry yeast	¼ cup wheat germ (optional)
¼ cup warm water	3½ - 4 cups all-purpose flour
¼ teaspoon sugar	

In a 10-inch Dutch oven scald the milk. Add the butter and honey and allow to cool to lukewarm. Dissolve the yeast with the sugar in ¼ cup warm water in a cup or small bowl. Add the wheat germ to the sourdough mixture. Combine the yeast mixture, sourdough mixture and the remaining ingredients. Beat well to mix. Add enough white flour to make a soft dough. Turn out onto a lightly floured surface and knead 8 to 10 times, adding flour if needed. Divide into half and form into loaves. Place into a 16-inch Dutch oven and let rise until almost double. Bake over a 375° fire for 35-40 minutes. Makes 2 loaves.

Sourdough French Bread

1¼ cups warm water
½ teaspoon soda
2 teaspoons salt
2 teaspoons sugar

1 cup starter
1 pkg. dry yeast
about 2 cups flour
4 cups unsifted flour

Pour the warm water into a large mixing bowl. Stir in the yeast. Add the starter, 4 cups flour, salt and sugar. Stir vigorously for about 3 minutes with a wooden spoon. Turn into a large greased bowl and let rise in a warm place until doubled in bulk (about 1½ hours). Mix soda with 1 cup of the remaining flour and stir in. The dough will be very stiff. Turn dough out onto a floured board and begin kneading. Add remaining flour. Knead 5 to 8 minutes. Shape into two oblong loaves or one large round one. Place in a lightly greased 16-inch Dutch oven, cover and let rise to nearly double in size. Make diagonal slashes across the loaf with a sharp knife. Mist the outside of the loaf before baking and every 10 to 15 minutes of cooking time. Bake over a 400° fire for 45 to 50 minutes or until golden brown. Makes 2 loaves.

Cottage Cheese Sourdough Bread
Rosemary Parkinson and Peggy Roskelley

1 tablespoon dry yeast
2 cups warm water
¾ cup sourdough starter
1 cup creamed cottage
  cheese
½ cup grated sharp or
  longhorn cheese

2 tablespoons fresh chopped
  onion
1 tablespoon cooking oil
1 tablespoon salt
1 tablespoon fresh dill,
  chopped
3 - 4 cups all-purpose flour

Dissolve yeast in warm water. Measure sourdough starter into a large mixing bowl. Add cheeses, dill, onion, oil, sugar and salt to starter. Add the dissolved yeast. Gradually beat in the flour ½ cup at a time, stirring well after each addition. Reserve

½ cup flour to work into the dough during kneading. The dough should be fairly stiff. Turn out onto a lightly floured surface and knead for 5 to 10 minutes, adding reserved flour if necessary. Put in a greased bowl, turning once. Cover with a cloth. Set in a warm place free from drafts and let rise for 2 hours or until doubled in size. Punch down the dough and shape into 3 ropes and braid. Cover with a cloth. Set in a warm place and let rise until doubled in size. It is wise to have the coals almost ready when the bread is ready to rise. Bake in a 14-inch Dutch oven with about 12 coals on the bottom and 18 on the lid for about 35 minutes. Makes one braid.

Holiday Bread

¼ cup warm water
2 cups unsifted flour
½ cup sugar
2 egg yolks
1 teaspoon salt
½ teaspoon cinnamon
1 cup unsifted flour
egg whites

½ cup sourdough starter
½ cup butter or margarine
1 cup unsifted flour
½ teaspoon soda
½ teaspoon grated lemon peel
½ cup sliced walnuts
½ cup raisins
½ cup fruit mix

Mix the water, starter and 2 cups flour in a mixing bowl. Cover and leave overnight at room temperature. The next morning cream the butter, sugar and egg yolks together with an egg beater or wire whip. Combine 1 cup flour, salt, soda, cinnamon and grated lemon peel. Blend into creamed mixture. Blend in the nuts, raisins and fruit mix. Mix with the starter mixture and pour out as a mound on the remaining 1 cup flour. Knead until satiny and not sticky. Add more flour if necessary. Divide dough in thirds and roll each third on a floured board with your hand to form a strand 18 inches long. Place strands in a 16-inch Dutch oven and form a straight braid. Let raise in a warm place for about 2 hours. Paint with the egg whites. Bake 45-50 minutes over a 350° fire. Makes one braid.

Honey Gold Bread

Make 1 quart of basic batter and let sit overnight.

2 cups milk
2 tablespoons butter
¼ cup honey
1 tablespoon active dry
   yeast
2 cups whole wheat flour

¼ cup wheat germ (optional)
2 tablespoons sugar
2 teaspoons salt
1 teaspoon baking soda
4 cups white flour

Scald the milk. Stir in the butter and honey. Allow to cool to lukewarm. Add yeast and stir until dissolved. Add this mix to the 1 quart basic sourdough batter. Add 2 cups wheat flour and wheat germ and stir until well mixed. Blend sugar, salt and soda until smooth. Sprinkle over the top of the dough and stir in gently. Set dough in a warm spot. Cover and let rise for 30 minutes. Stir down and add the remaining flour as needed until dough is stiff. Turn out on a floured board and begin to knead with hands until dough is light and satiny. Mold into loaves and let rise. Bake over a 400° fire for 20 minutes then reduce temperature to 325° and bake until done (30 minutes). Makes 2 loaves.

Chapter 9

Beef Entrees

Chili

1 pound hamburger
1 large onion, chopped
2 cloves garlic, crushed
1 can (16 oz.) whole tomatoes
2 medium stalks celery,
 sliced
1 tablespoon chili powder

2 teaspoons salt
1 teaspoon sugar
1 teaspoon Worcestershire
 sauce
½ teaspoon red pepper sauce
1 can (15 oz.) kidney beans,
 drained

Cook and stir hamburger, onion and garlic in a 10-inch Dutch oven until hamburger is light brown; drain. Stir in tomatoes (with liquid), celery, chili powder, salt, sugar, Worcestershire sauce and pepper sauce. Heat to boiling; reduce heat. Cover and simmer 1 hour. Stir in beans. Heat to boiling; reduce heat. Simmer uncovered until hot, about 15 minutes. (For thicker chili, continue simmering, stirring occasionally, until desired consistency.) Makes 5 servings (about 1 cup each).

Spaghetti

2 medium onions, chopped
3 cloves garlic, minced
½ cup chopped parsley
2 tablespoons salad oil
2 pounds ground beef
3 cans (16 oz.) tomatoes
3 cans (6 oz.) tomato paste
2 tablespoons sugar

4 teaspoons salt
2 teaspoons oregano leaves
¼ teaspoon ground black
  pepper
1 bay leaf
2½ pounds spaghetti, cooked
  and drained
grated parmesan or romano
  cheese

In a 12-inch Dutch oven, saute onion, garlic and parsley in oil until tender but not browned. Add meat, stirring to break up the meat as it browns. Crush tomatoes with a potato masher. Add to Dutch oven along with tomato paste, sugar, salt, oregano, basil, pepper and bay leaf. Bring to a boil; stir well. Cover and simmer 30 minutes, stirring occasionally. Serve 1 cup of sauce for each portion of spaghetti. Pass grated cheese separately. Makes 8 servings.

Sukiyaki

1½ lb. steak, cut in thin strips
2 teaspoons salad oil
¼ cup sugar
¾ cup soy sauce
2 medium onions sliced
1 green pepper, in thin strips
1 cup (1½ inch) strips celery
1 can bamboo shoots, sliced thin
1 can mushrooms, sliced thin
1 bunch green onions, cut 1″ long including tops

Heat oil in a 10- or 12-inch Dutch oven. Add meat and brown lightly. Mix sugar, soy sauce, and mushroom stock. Cook half of this with meat. Push meat to one side of pan and add sliced onions, green peppers, and celery. Keep separated. Cook a few minutes; add remaining soy sauce mixture, bamboo shoots, and mushrooms. Cook 3 to 5 minutes. Add green onions. Cook 1 minute more. Serve immediately over hot rice. Makes 4 servings. NOTE: Thinly sliced carrots, bean threads (an oriental ingredient that looks like clear spaghetti), or fresh vegetables that your family likes may be added.

Hungarian Goulash

2 pounds beef for stew, cut into 1-inch cubes
1 medium onion, sliced
1 small clove garlic, finely chopped, or ⅛ teaspoon instant minced garlic
¼ cup shortening
1½ cups water
2 teaspoons paprika
½ teaspoon dry mustard
¾ cup catsup
2 tablespoons Worcestershire sauce
1 tablespoon packed brown sugar
2 teaspoons salt
dash cayenne red pepper
¼ cup cold water
2 tablespoons flour
noodles

In a 10-inch Dutch oven, cook and stir beef, onion and garlic in shortening until beef is browned. Drain off any excess grease. Stir in 1½ cups water, catsup, Worcestershire sauce, brown sugar, salt, paprika, mustard and red pepper. Heat to boiling; reduce heat. Cover and simmer until beef is tender, 2 to 2½ hours. Shake ¼ cup cold water and the flour in tightly covered container; stir gradually into beef mixture. Heat to boiling, stirring constantly. Boil and stir 1 minute. Serve over hot noodles. Makes 6 to 8 servings.

No Alarm Chili
Val and Marie Cowley

4 large onions (chopped
1½ green peppers (chopped)
5 pounds lean beef (cubed)
¼ cup margarine or butter

Melt butter and brown meat. Add onions and green peppers. Cook until tender.

Add:

1 clove garlic
8 bay leaves
1 tablespoon salt
2 tablespoons chili powder
4 cups tomato sauce
2 tablespoons bouillon cubes
¾ teaspoon red pepper

½ cup red wine vinegar
1 tablespoon paprika
1½ tablespoons cumin
½ teaspoon black pepper
½ teaspoon Accent (MSG)
1 tablespoon oregano
1 - 7 oz. can green chilies (sliced)

Simmer together 2 to 3 hours or until desired thickness. Garnish with hot peppers. Makes 12-15 servings.

Chimichangas

1 doz. large flour tortillas
1 can green chilies, chopped
3 medium tomatoes, diced
sour cream for garnish
2 onions, chopped

dash of salt, pepper, and garlic salt
2 lbs. lean meat, cubed
2-3 tablespoons flour
2 cups oil

Heat ¼ cup oil in a 12-inch Dutch oven. Brown meat. Add onions and cook till soft. Add flour to thicken. Add tomatoes, chilies, salt and pepper and garlic salt to taste. Add just enough water to cover, and simmer till mixture thickens. Set aside. When mixture is a little cool, spoon on tortillas and roll up. Then deep fry in a Dutch oven till golden brown. Garnish with sour cream or guacamole. Makes 12 servings.

Chapter 10

Pork Entrees

Orange Glazed Pork Roast

4 to 5 pound boneless pork loin roast
   (double loin, rolled, tied)
1½ teaspoons ginger
¼ cup frozen orange juice concentrate, thawed
¼ cup honey
orange and lime slices, fresh pineapple spears
   and watercress, optional garnish

Combine orange juice concentrate, honey and remaining ½ teaspoon ginger. Bring to boil; boil 1 minute. Cool slightly and pour into a bowl and reserve. Rub surface of roast with 1 teaspoon ginger. Place roast in Dutch oven. Insert meat thermometer so bulb is in center of thickest part of roast. Roast on 350° fire about 2½ hours or until meat thermometer registers 170°F. Brush sauce over roast several times during the last 30 minutes of cooking time. Let stand 15 minutes before slicing. Garnish with orange and lime slices, pineapple spears and watercress, if desired. Makes 8 to 10 servings.

Pork Tamale Bake

1 pound ground pork
¾ cup chopped onion
½ cup chopped green pepper
1 teaspoon salt
¼ teaspoon pepper
2 to 3 teaspoons chili powder
1 can (16 ounces) tomatoes
1 can (12 ounces) whole kernel corn
Cornbread Topping (recipe below)

Lightly brown pork, onion and green pepper in a 10-inch Dutch oven. Add salt, pepper, chili powder, tomatoes and corn. Bring to boil; simmer 8 minutes, stirring occasionally. Meanwhile, make Cornbread Topping. Spread the pork mixture evenly in the Dutch oven. Spoon Cornbread Topping over hot pork mixture. Bake over a 375° fire, 30 to 40 minutes. Makes 6 servings.

Cornbread Topping

1 cup corn meal
1 teaspoon baking powder
1 teaspoon sugar
½ teaspoon salt
2 tablespoons finely chopped onion
1 egg, beaten

In bowl, combine ingredients. Stir only to moisten cornmeal.

Fruit Glazed Shoulder Roast

3 to 4 pounds pork shoulder roast
2 lemons
2 oranges
1 grapefruit
1 cup sugar
1 cup water
garlic salt

Place unpeeled lemons, oranges and grapefruit in a 12 inch Dutch oven. Cover with water and bring to a boil. Boil 30 minutes. Remove the fruit from the Dutch oven and cut into sections. In the Dutch oven, stir together liquid, sugar and 1 cup water; boil 5 minutes. Place fruit sections in the Dutch oven with the syrup. Cover and bake for 1½ hours over a 325° fire. Rub roast with garlic salt. Insert meat thermometer at an angle so the tip is in center of roast but not touching bone. After 10 to 15 minutes of cooking, begin to brush on glaze. Roast over a 350° fire for 2½ hours or until meat thermometer registers 170°F. Serve fruit glaze with roast. Makes 10 to 12 servings.

Apple-Orange Stuffed Pork Chops

6 pork loin chops, cut 1½-inches thick
½ cup chopped celery
½ cup chopped unpeeled apple
2 tablespoons butter
1½ cups toasted raisin bread cubes
1 orange, sectioned and chopped
1 beaten egg
½ teaspoon grated orange peel
¼ teaspoon salt
⅛ teaspoon ground cinnamon

Cut a pocket in each pork chop by cutting to center of chop from rib side parallel to rib bone and surface of chop. Cook celery and apple in butter in a 12-inch Dutch oven. Toss with remaining ingredients. Spoon about ¼ cup stuffing into each slitted chop; secure opening with toothpicks. Bake on a 350° fire until done, about 30 to 40 minutes. Makes 6 servings.

Chapter 11

Lamb Entrees

Baked Breast of Lamb

3 pounds breast of lamb
1 teaspoon whole cloves
¼ cup honey

¼ cup lemon juice
1 teaspoon salt

Place lamb breasts in a 10- or 12-inch Dutch oven. Roast 1 hour and 45 minutes. Drain off excess fat. Combine cloves, honey, lemon juice and salt; then pour over lamb. Bake about 20 minutes more.
Makes 10-12 servings.

Sweet and Sour Lamb Stew

1 can (8¾ ounces) pineapple tidbits
1 green pepper, sliced
½ cup diagonally sliced celery
½ cup vinegar
½ cup sugar
1 teaspoon soy sauce
1 tablespoon cornstarch
2 tablespoons water
3 pounds neck slices cut up, well browned until done
1 whole pimento, sliced
hot cooked rice

Drain pineapple, reserving syrup. In a 10-inch Dutch oven, combine green pepper, celery, syrup, vinegar, sugar and Kikkoman soy sauce; stir and bring to a boil. Blend cornstarch with water; add to the Dutch oven and boil ½ minute, stirring constantly. Add lamb, pineapple tidbits and pimento; heat thoroughly. Serve over rice. Makes 8 servings.

Peggy's Lamb
Peggy Roskelley and Rosemary Parkinson

3 to 4 pound leg of lamb
1 clove garlic
2 teaspoons fresh marjoram
½ teaspoon salt

2 tablespoons lemon juice
½ teaspoon tabasco
2 strips fatty bacon
1 bottle small stuffed green olives

Mash and mix garlic, marjoram, and salt together. Add lemon juice and tabasco. Cut bacon into ½ inch pieces. Cut excess fat off lamb and wipe with clean damp cloth. Make 10 holes with sharp narrow knife as far as you can cut without cutting through meat. Push small olive in hole, then a piece of bacon, ½ teaspoon of garlic mixture, then another stuffed olive until all holes are filled. Roast with about 10 briquettes on bottom and 18 briquettes on top for 3 hours or until done. Keep the briquettes on the outer rim of the lid. Garnish with parsley, or serve with stir-fry vegetables heaped around meat in the Dutch oven. Makes 10-12 servings.

Moussaka

1 pound ground lamb
1 tablespoon parsley, chopped
1 teaspoon salt
⅛ teaspoon pepper
⅛ teaspoon nutmeg
1 medium onion, chopped

¼ cup water
16 oz. can tomatoes, drained
1 medium eggplant
2 eggs
¼ cup milk
¼ cup parmesan cheese, grated

In a 10-inch Dutch oven, brown lamb. Drain excess fat. Add parsley, salt, pepper, nutmeg, onion, water and tomatoes. Pour contents from the Dutch oven. Peel eggplant and slice crosswise in one-quarter-inch slices. Arrange half of the eggplant slices in the bottom of the 10-inch Dutch oven. Top with half of the meat mixture. Place the remaining eggplant as the next layer, finishing with the last of the meat mixture. Bake over a 375° fire for about 40 minutes or until eggplant is tender. Beat the eggs and milk together; pour over the partially baked casserole. Sprinkle with cheese. Return to the fire and bake for 10 to 15 minutes or until egg mixture is set. Let stand about 10 minutes before serving. Makes 6-8 servings.

Chapter 12

Chicken Entrees

Roast Chicken with Cream Cheese and Herb Stuffing

1 roaster chicken (3-4 lb.)
2 cloves garlic peeled and crushed
¼ cube butter

stuffing:
1 8-ounce package cream cheese
1 egg yolk
1 small onion
½-1 tablespoon chopped chives or rosemary
2 tablespoons sour cream
1 cup soft bread crumbs
3 tablespoons chopped parsley

Beat cream cheese, sour cream, egg into bread crumbs. Stir into onions and herbs, season to taste with salt and pepper. Stuff chicken. Mix garlic to a paste with salt and pepper, then spread on chicken. Put in a 12-inch Dutch oven. Bake over a 350° fire for 1¼-1½ hours or until done. Makes 4-6 servings.

How to Bone a Chicken
Place the chicken on the table with the back up and the neck facing away from you. With a sharp knife, start at the neck

and cut the skin down to the bone along the backbone to the tail. Remove the tail. Take a corner of the skin where the tail was cut off and start to trim the skin and meat away from the bones. Be *very careful* not to shave small slivers of bone off into the meat. Strip the meat down to where the thigh bone is attached. Pop the thigh bone out of the socket and cut the tendons. Continue stripping the meat down the side of the bird to where the ribs from the front and back meet. Continue separating the meat along the side of the bird, up to the wing. Dislocate the wing bone out of the socket and cut the tendons, the same as for the thigh. Cut the breast meat away from the wishbone. Repeat the process on the other side. When completed, continue removing the meat from the ribs to the cartilage of the breast. Fillet the breast meat off the cartilage. Turn the bird and repeat the boning process on the other side. All the bones should be removed now except the thigh and wing bones. Take hold of one of the thigh bones at the large end that is exposed. Using your knife, peel the meat away from the bone, turning the meat inside out as you go. (The skin is on the inside and the meat on the outside.) Cut around the joint leading to the drumstick. Peel the meat away from the drumstick all the way down to the end. Cut the bones free from the skin. Remove the other thigh bone in the same manner. The wing bones are the only bones that are not removed.

Boneless Stuffed Chicken

2 whole fryers
very sharp knife
needle and dark thread
1 cube butter or margarine
1 large onion, diced
giblets, cut up
1 chicken bouillon cube
salt and pepper to taste

poultry seasoning to taste
½ loaf of bread, cut into
    ½-inch pieces
1 cup grated carrots
1 cup diced green peppers
1 cup chopped parsley
1 egg

Melt the butter in the Dutch oven. Add the onion, giblets, bouillon cube, and spices. Saute for 5 minutes or until the giblets are cooked. (Make sure the bouillon cube dissolves.) Add the bread pieces, carrots, green peppers, parsley and egg. Mix well. If the stuffing is too dry, add some water. If the stuffing is too moist, add more bread pieces. Set aside.

Bone the chicken as explained in the accompanying directions. Salt the inside of the chicken lightly. Starting at the neck opening, take the needle and thread (dark thread is best so you can find it to remove before serving) and whip stitch the skin closed across the neck cavity, down the back to the vent area. When you reach the vent area, stop stitching and stuff the bird with the stuffing. Be careful not to stuff the bird too full or it will fall apart when cooked. Also, stuff the thighs and legs. Complete sewing the skin closed. Arrange the chickens in a 12-inch Dutch oven. Cover and place on a 350° fire (7-8 briquettes on the bottom and 13-15 on the lid). Baste with the drippings each time you check it.

When completely cooked (approximately 1½ hours) remove all the drippings from the pan and pull the thread out that was used to sew the skin closed. Makes 4-6 servings.

Chicken Pot Pie

⅓ cup margarine, butter or chicken fat
⅓ cup all purpose flour
⅓ cup onion, chopped
½ teaspoon salt
¼ teaspoon pepper
1¾ cups chicken or turkey broth
⅔ cup milk
2 cups cooked chicken or turkey, cut up
1 package (10 oz.) frozen peas and carrots
Celery Seed Pastry (below)

In an 8-inch Dutch oven heat the margarine until melted. Blend in flour, onion, salt and pepper. Continue cooking, stirring constantly, until mixture is smooth and bubbly; remove from heat. Stir in broth and milk. Heat to boiling, stirring constantly. Boil and stir 1 minute. Stir in chicken and frozen vegetables; reserve this mixture for later.

Prepare celery seed pastry. Roll ⅔ of the pastry into a cool 8-inch Dutch oven. Place the crust in the oven as described in the section on pies. Put the filling inside the crust, then roll out and put on the top crust. Seal edges and flute. Cut slits in the center of the top crust to allow the steam to escape. Bake over a 400° to 425° fire until the crust is brown. Makes 8 servings.

Celery Seed Pastry

⅔ cup plus 2 tablespoons shortening or ⅔ cup lard
2 cups all-purpose flour
2 teaspoons celery seed
1 teaspoon salt
4 to 5 tablespoons water

Cut shortening into flour, celery seed and salt until particles are the size of small peas. Sprinkle in water, 1 tablespoon at a time, tossing with fork until all flour is moistened and pastry almost cleans the side of the bowl (1 to 2 teaspoons water can be added if necessary). Gather pastry into a ball.

Malibu Chicken

3 whole chicken breasts, skinned and boned
¾ cup crushed corn flakes
6 thin slices of ham
6 thin slices of Swiss cheese
3 tablespoons butter or margarine, melted

Cut chicken breast in half lengthwise. Place each half between two layers of waxed paper or plastic wrap. Using a meat mallet or other heavy object, pound the breast to a 7 inch by

4 inch rectangle. Pour corn flakes into a pie plate and set aside. Alternate ham and cheese slices on one side of chicken, then fold over the other side. Brush melted butter evenly over chicken and roll in the crushed corn flakes. Arrange in a 12-inch Dutch oven and bake over a 350° fire until done. Serve with melted cheese on the top or with a mustard sauce. Makes 6 servings.

Hawaiian Luau Chicken

1 fryer, cut up, or 3 chicken breasts
1 large #2 can pineapple
½ cup brown sugar
2 tablespoons cornstarch
½ teaspoon salt
½ cup vinegar
1 tablespoon soy sauce
½ medium onion, chopped
½ medium green pepper
½ to 1 pound fresh mushrooms

Skin the chicken. In a 12-inch Dutch oven brown the chicken in ¼ cup butter or cooking oil for 20 minutes. Cover the oven and continue cooking until the chicken is cooked clear through. Push the chicken to the side and make the sauce in the same pan. Drain the pineapple and mix the sugar, cornstarch, salt, vinegar, and juice. Stir until thick. Combine the remaining ingredients and simmer over a small fire for 15 to 20 minutes. Serve over rice. Makes 3-6 servings.

Chicken Spaghetti
Paul and Kathy Stewart

breasts from 2 chickens (or 1 whole chicken)
5 16-ounce cans of tomato sauce
1 medium onion, chopped
8 ounces fresh mushrooms, chopped
2 28-ounce cans whole tomatoes, chopped

¼ cup Schilling Italian Seasoning
2 to 3 cloves of garlic
2 tablespoons powder chicken bouillon
1 teaspoon sugar
½ cup water
1½ pounds spaghetti noodles

Bone the chicken and cut into bite-size pieces. Place chicken into a 12-inch Dutch oven along with ½ cup of water, a sprinkle of garlic powder, onion powder, and Italian Seasoning. Stir occasionally until done. Add tomato sauce, onion, mushrooms, whole tomatoes (chopped), rest of Italian Seasoning, garlic, bouillon and sugar. Simmer 30 minutes, stirring occasionally. Empty sauce into a bowl and begin layering uncooked spaghetti noodles and sauce. Always begin and end with sauce. After each layer of sauce be sure to mash down lightly with a spoon. Cook an additional 30 to 45 minutes until noodles are done. Stir occasionally. Makes 12-15 servings.

Gefueltes Huhn
David and Irene Johnson

1 small roasting chicken	1 teaspoon salt
	¼ teaspoon marjoram
Stuffing:	
1 cup fine white bread crumbs	3 tablespoons melted butter
2 egg yolks	½ teaspoon salt
1 egg white	some freshly ground pepper
1 cup heavy cream	8 cooked shrimp
2 tablespoons green peas	½ cup butter

Pour the cream over the bread crumbs and allow to soak. Add the 3 tablespoons of melted butter. Cook slowly for about 10 minutes. Beat the egg yolks in a basin, add the salt and pepper. Now add this to the bread crumb mixture. Chop the shrimp and stir them into the stuffing. Add the green peas and finally add the white of egg beaten stiffly.

Wash the chicken quickly under cold running water. Pat it dry with paper towels, then rub the inside with a mixture of the salt and marjoram. Stuff the breast only with the above stuffing and fold the breast skin over and secure it to keep the dressing in. Place the chicken in a 12-inch Dutch oven, breast up. Pour the ½ cup of melted butter over the whole bird. Bake for 45 minutes to 1 hour, depending on the size and age of the bird. Baste it frequently with pan juices.
Makes 4-6 servings.

5 Cheese Chicken Breasts
Don and Sally Carrier

8 boned and skinned chicken breasts
8 thin slices mozzarella cheese
8 thin slices Swiss cheese
½ cup ricotta cheese
1 tablespoon grated parmesan cheese
1 egg yolk
1 cup all purpose flour
1 egg beaten
½ cup bread crumbs
1 tablespoon oil
1 tablespoon butter

Place the 8 chicken breasts between pieces of plastic wrap and flatten with a mallet from the center out to form thin cutlets. On each cutlet place a slice each of mozzarella and Swiss cheese. Mix ricotta and parmesan cheeses with egg yolk. Divide among cutlets, placing a spoonful at the wide end of each cutlet. Roll up cutlets from wide end, secure with toothpick and roll each in flour, dip in egg and coat with crumbs. Brown chicken on both sides in hot oil and butter in the bottom of a 12-inch Dutch oven with 15 briquettes on the bottom. When all breasts are browned, place the lid on top of the Dutch oven and place 10 of the 15 briquettes on the top and leave 5 briquettes on the bottom. Cook for 20 minutes, rotating the oven every 5 minutes. When done cooking put chicken breasts on the lid. Remove the toothpicks and cover with Cheddar Cheese Sauce (following recipe). Makes 8 servings.

Cheddar Cheese Sauce

2 tablespoons melted butter
2 tablespoons dry sherry
2 tablespoons all-purpose flour
1 cup grated sharp cheddar cheese
1¼ cups milk
½ teaspoon Worcestershire sauce
1 tablespoon dry parsley flakes

Melt 2 tablespoons butter in a small Dutch oven. Stir in the flour. Add the milk and cook, stirring until thickened. Stir in Worcestershire sauce, dry sherry and sharp cheese. Pour over chicken breasts and sprinkle with parsley flakes.

Southern Fried Chicken

1 fryer, 2 to 3 pounds
2 cups evaporated milk
2 cups flour
salt and pepper

enough shortening to make
an inch in the bottom of
a 10-inch Dutch oven

Dip the chicken pieces in the evaporated milk and then in the flour which contains the salt and pepper. Brown the chicken on both sides in a 10-inch Dutch oven. Lower the heat and cover. Continue cooking for 25 minutes or until done when checked with a fork. Turn the chicken as it cooks if needed. Makes 6-8 servings.

Barbecued Chicken and Ribs

2 whole chickens, skinned
and cut up
2-4 pounds ribs (I like both
beef and pork)
2 onions chopped

1 cup brown sugar
2 cups water
1 cup vinegar
4 cups catsup
salt and pepper to taste

Saute onions in a little bit of oil until they are just tender. Add the rest of the ingredients for the sauce. Let it simmer uncovered until it gets thick. Add the ribs and cook uncovered or at least partially uncovered for about one hour. Add the chicken and cook for about 1½-2 hours or until tender. If you want the meat to cook faster, leave the lid on the Dutch oven. However, this will make the sauce runny so when the meat is through cooking thicken the sauce with cornstarch. Makes 12-15 servings.

Chapter 13

Cakes, Brownies and Fudge

Cake Baking Hints and Tips

Mix together a cake mix or a cake from scratch as the directions indicate. Pour into a greased 12-inch Dutch oven. Making sure the oven is level, place the oven over 8 briquettes and place 14 briquettes on the lid. A tilted oven will cause part of the cake to bake faster than the other side. To prevent hot spots rotate the oven and the lid each one-quarter turn every 5 to 10 minutes. Be careful not to jar the oven sharply or your cake may fall. Check the cake after 15 to 20 minutes to make sure it isn't cooking too fast.

When done, the cake will spring back when touched. Let the cake rest for a few minutes then turn out on the lid. If you prefer not to turn the cake out on the lid, take the cake off the heat source before it is completely cooked. Cast-iron Dutch ovens retain heat and will continue to cook the cake, giving it a burned taste. Frost when cool and enjoy.

Fruit and Nut Cobbler Cake

1 can pie filling
1 can crushed pineapple
1 white or yellow cake mix
½ cup butter or margarine
nuts

Place fruit in the bottom of a 12-inch Dutch oven. Spread the dry cake mix over the fruit. Cut the butter into small pieces and sprinkle over the cake mix. If desired, add a layer of nuts, either chopped or whole. Bake over a 350° fire for 1 hour or until done. Serve hot. Makes 12-15 servings.

Variations:
Add raisins to the fruit
Use different flavored cake mixes

Brownie Pudding Cake

1½ cups sifted flour
1 cup sugar
3 tablespoons cocoa
3 teaspoons baking powder
¼ teaspoon salt
½ cup brown sugar
¼ cup sugar

3 tablespoons cocoa
¾ cup milk
1½ tablespoons melted butter
2 teaspoons vanilla
¾ cup chopped walnuts
1¾ cups boiling water
vanilla ice cream

Sift together flour, 1 cup sugar, 3 tablespoons cocoa, baking powder and salt into a bowl. Add milk, butter and vanilla; beat well. Stir in walnuts. Spread batter in a greased 12-inch Dutch oven. Combine brown sugar, ¼ cup sugar and remaining 3 tablespoons cocoa. Sprinkle over batter. Pour boiling water over all. Bake over a 350° fire for 40 minutes or until cake tests done. Serve warm, topped with vanilla ice cream. Makes 12-15 servings.

Hot Fudge Pudding Cake

1 cup buttermilk baking mix
1 cup sugar
3 tablespoons plus ⅓ cup
   unsweetened cocoa powder

1 teaspoon vanilla
1⅔ cup hot tap water
powdered sugar (optional)
½ cup milk

Mix buttermilk baking mix, ½ cup sugar and 3 tablespoons cocoa. Stir in milk and vanilla until well blended. Pour into a greased 10-inch Dutch oven. Sprinkle remaining ⅓ cup cocoa and ½ cup sugar evenly over the surface of the batter. Pour the water over the top. Bake over a 350° fire for 40 minutes or until top is firm. Dust with powdered sugar. Makes 12-15 servings.

Fruit Cocktail Cake

1½ cups sugar
2 cups flour
¼ teaspoon salt
1 can fruit cocktail (juice and all)

2 beaten eggs
1 teaspoon soda
1 teaspoon vanilla

Mix and pour into a 12-inch Dutch oven. Crumble ½ cup brown sugar and ½ cup chopped nuts over the top. Bake over a 350° fire for 45 minutes or until the cake springs back when touched. Makes 12-15 servings.

In a 10-inch Dutch oven (or smaller) boil ¼ cups sugar, 1 stick margarine and ½ cup canned milk for 3 minutes and pour over the top of the cake.

Zucchini Brownies

2 cups grated zucchini
1½ cups sugar
1½ teaspoons soda
2 teaspoons vanilla

2 cups flour
1 teaspoon salt
scant ¼ cup cocoa
½ cup oil

Put all dry ingredients together in a bowl. Mix well. Add the remaining ingredients. Pour into a greased 12-inch Dutch oven and bake over a 350° fire for 25 minutes or until done. Makes 12-15 servings.

Baked Fudge Cake
Mike and Peggy Nath

1½ cups sifted all-purpose flour
3 heaping teaspoons baking powder
1⅛ teaspoons salt
¾ cup sugar
1⅛ cups chopped nuts
¾ cup milk
1½ teaspoons vanilla
3 tablespoons melted margarine or shortening
3 tablespoons cocoa

Topping

¼ cup cocoa
¾ cup brown sugar, packed
1 teaspoon vanilla
1¾ cups hot/boiling water

Lightly grease the bottom and sides of a 12-inch Dutch oven. Sift the first 5 ingredients into a bowl. Stir in nuts, milk, vanilla and margarine. Spread in the greased oven.

Mix cocoa and brown sugar. Sprinkle over batter in oven. Add vanilla to water; pour gently over all. Bake in moderate oven (350°) for 45 to 50 minutes (6 to 8 coals on bottom, 12 to 14 coals on top).

Can be served warm or cold; with whipped cream or ice cream. Makes 12-15 servings.

Sourdough Chocolate-Cherry Cake
Nan and Steve Hasler

1 can pitted sour pie cherries
    (in water) 16 oz.
about ¼ cup milk
½ cup sourdough starter
    (at room temperature)
1½ cups all-purpose flour
1 cup sliced almonds
⅔ cup butter

1 cup sugar
2 large eggs
¼ teaspoon cinnamon
¼ teaspoon nutmeg
¼ teaspoon almond extract
½ cup unsweetened cocoa
1½ teaspoons baking soda
½ cup semi-sweet chocolate
chips

Drain cherries well, saving the liquid. Add enough milk to the liquid to make 1 cup. In a bowl, mix starter, liquid mixture and 1 cup of flour. Place almonds in an 8-inch Dutch oven and bake over a 350° fire until golden brown. Set aside.

In a large mixing blow, beat butter and sugar until well combined. Beat in eggs one at a time with the cinnamon, nutmeg and almond extract. Sift the remaining ½ cup flour, cocoa and soda into the butter mixture. Beat until smooth. Add starter mixture and beat well. Stir in almonds, cherries and chocolate chips.

Grease a 12-inch Dutch oven well. Spread batter evenly in the oven. Bake over a 350° fire until all sides pull away from the oven. Serve warm or cool. If desired, sift powdered sugar on top of the cake and garnish with cherry pie filling. Makes 12-15 servings.

Prize Chocolate Cake

¼ cup butter
1 teaspoon vanilla
¾ teaspoon baking soda
1¾ cups unsifted all-purpose flour
1¾ cup milk

2 cups sugar
2 eggs
¾ cup cocoa
⅛ teaspoon salt

Cream the butter, shortening, sugar and vanilla until light and fluffy. Blend in the eggs. Combine baking soda, cocoa, flour, baking powder and salt in a bowl. Add alternately with milk to the batter. Blend well. Pour into a greased and floured 12-inch Dutch oven. Bake over a 350° fire for 30 to 35 minutes or until it tests done. Turn the cake out on the lid to cool. Makes 12-15 servings.

Oatmeal Cake

½ cup butter or margarine
1 cup brown sugar
1 cup white sugar
2 eggs
1½ cups sifted flour
1 teaspoon baking powder

1 cup oatmeal

1 teaspoon baking soda
1 teaspoon salt
2 teaspoons cinnamon
1 teaspoon nutmeg
½ teaspoon cardamon
   (optional)
1 teaspoon vanilla

1½ cups boiling water

Let the oatmeal and boiling water soak for 20 minutes. Cream the butter and sugars together. Add eggs and beat well. Add the oatmeal. Sift the dry ingredients. Add and mix well. Pour into a well greased 12-inch Dutch oven and bake over a 350° fire until the cake springs back when touched. Makes 12-15 servings.

Icing

   1 cup brown sugar
   ½ cup milk
   ⅓ cup butter

Cook together about 3 minutes. Add 1 cup chopped walnuts and 1 cup flaked coconut. Cool and spread on the cake in the Dutch oven or on the lid.

Carrot Pineapple Cake

1½ cups sifted flour
1 cup sugar
1 teaspoon baking powder
1 teaspoon soda
1 teaspoon salt
1 teaspoon cinnamon

½ teaspoon nutmeg
1 teaspoon vanilla
⅔ cup shortening or butter
2 eggs
1 cup finely shredded carrots
½ cup crushed pineapple
   with juice

Cream butter and sugar until light. Add eggs and beat well. Sift dry ingredients together and add with pineapple. Beat well to mix. Bake in a well greased 12-inch Dutch oven over a 350° fire until the top of the cake springs back when touched. Makes 12-15 servings.

White Cake

6 egg whites, beaten
1 teaspoon cream of tartar
⅔ cup sugar
1 cup butter
1⅓ cups sugar
1 teaspoon vanilla

1 teaspoon lemon extract
½ teaspoon almond extract
3 cups sifted cake flour
1 teaspoon baking powder
1 teaspoon soda
1 teaspoon salt

Beat the egg whites until stiff. Add the cream of tartar and ⅔ cup of sugar. Cream together the butter, 1⅓ cups sugar, vanilla, lemon extract and almond extract until light. Sift the remaining dry ingredients together three times. Add one-third of the dry ingredients at a time to the creamed mixture with 1¼ cup buttermilk. Mix well after each addition. Fold in beaten egg whites last. Bake in a greased and floured 16-inch Dutch oven over a 350° fire until done. Do not overcook. Makes 12-15 servings.

Festival Fudge

1 stick butter (¼ pound)
1 can evaporated milk
5 cups sugar
2 cups chocolate pieces
1 cup chopped nuts
1 heaping cup marshmallow

Set oven on coals and melt butter covering the complete inside of the oven as it melts. Add the milk and sugar. Cook and stir until it thickens and makes a suction noise when you stir it. (NOTE: Stir slowly so you don't splash any of the sugar milk mixture on the sides of the Dutch oven. This will help decrease the chances of having the fudge go to sugar.)

Remove from the fire and pour the contents, without scraping the inside of the Dutch oven, into a large bowl with the chocolate pieces, nuts and marshmallow. Stir until it gets stiff and starts to set. Scrape bowl and pour into a greased or foil-lined small cookie sheet. Spread quickly and drop the pan once on the counter to level the fudge.

Chapter 14

Pies

Pie Baking Hints and Tips

Baking pies directly in a Dutch oven takes a little practice to master. The hardest part is to get the crust into the oven without it breaking apart. This can be accomplished by rolling the dough out ⅛" thick on top of plastic wrap. Now you can lift the dough up and handle it easily because it clings to the plastic wrap. Place the dough in a cool oven and press it into

Dutch oven apple pie.

place using the plastic wrap to keep the dough from sticking to your hands. Using a knife, cut away the excess dough that will not be needed and flute the edges.

To bake a single crust place the oven over 8 briquettes for 4 minutes. Move the oven immediately from the bottom heat and place 40 coals on the lid and cook until the shell is well browned.

If you are baking a double crusted pie place the filling in the bottom shell, then roll out the top crust as you did the bottom one. Place on the pie and trim with a knife or kitchen scissors. Seal together with the bottom crust and flute the edges. Bake as you would a cake or rolls at the temperature indicated in the recipe.

If using a cast-iron Dutch oven don't let your crust get too dark before removing the oven from the fire. The pie will continue to brown after it has been taken from the fire because the iron retains the heat.

Apricot Almandine Pie

6 cups fresh apricots, pitted
1½ cups sugar
6 tablespoons flour
½ teaspoon nutmeg

½ teaspoon almond extract
½ cup slivered almonds
¼ cup butter
dash of salt

Mix sugar, flour, nutmeg and salt. Mix with fresh apricots. Add almond extract and almonds. Heap into pie shell and dot with butter. Place top crust. Crimp edges. Bake with 7-8 briquettes on the bottom and 15 briquettes on the top for 45-60 minutes. Makes 8-12 servings.

Grandma's Candied Apple Dumplings

Dean and Julie Hatch

8 medium apples
8 tablespoons butter

Pastry
1½ teaspoons salt
1⅓ cups shortening
1 tablespoon vinegar

Syrup
2 cups water
¼ pound butter

¾ cup sugar
2 teaspoons ground cinnamon

4 cups sifted flour
1 egg, beaten
8 tablespoons water

1 cup sugar
½ cup red hot candies

Peel apples and slice in thin slices.

Pastry:

Place flour and salt in bowl. Cut shortening into flour and salt with a pastry blender until pieces are the size of peas. Beat egg lightly in a 1½ cup measure; add vinegar and fill cup with ice cold water. Add just barely enough liquid to dry ingredients to hold dough together — about 6 to 7 tablespoons. Refrigerate the remaining liquid for the next batch of pastry. Handle dough as little as possible. Divide pastry into 8 equal pieces. Roll each piece to approximately ⅛″ thick, 8 to 9 inches in diameter.

Syrup:

Combine sugar, butter, water, and red hots. Heat to boiling and boil for three minutes. Pour into a bowl and set aside.

Mix ¾ cup sugar and 2 teaspoons cinnamon in a small bowl. Divide apples into eight equal portions. Place apples on pastry and sprinkle 1 tablespoon of sugar and cinnamon mixture on the apples. Place 1 tablespoon of butter on top of the apples and bring the pastry up and fold over the top of the apples. Place in a 14-inch Dutch oven. Pour hot syrup around the dumplings and cover with the lid. Place 8 coals on the bottom and 20 coals on the top of the Dutch oven and cook for 30 to 40 minutes or until apples are tender and the crust is browned on top.

Serve with ice cream, cool whip, or light cream. Makes 8-10 dumplings.

Open-Face Peach Pie

Ross and Angie Conlin

2½ cups flour
1 cup shortening
1 teaspoon salt
1 egg, beaten
1 tablespoon vinegar
¼ cup cold water

4½ pounds unpeeled peaches, pitted and sliced
1¼ cups sugar
1 cup sifted flour
4 tablespoons butter, cut into small pieces
2 tablespoons fresh lemon juice

Mix flour, shortening, and salt in a bowl and mix well with a fork. Add egg, vinegar, and cold water. Mix well and form into a ball. Flatten between wax paper and roll out to fit the Dutch oven and up the sides. Roll the top and pinch together. Bake in Dutch oven 15 minutes using 5 coals on the bottom and 10 on the top.

Arrange peaches in crust. Mix sugar and flour. Sprinkle over the peaches. Dot with small pieces of butter. Drizzle with lemon juice. Bake until peaches are tender, about 45 minutes. Use 8 coals on the bottom and 14 on top.

Serve with fresh blueberries and ice cream or whipped cream. Makes 8-12 servings.

Fresh Peach Pie

1 can frozen orange juice with:
      1½ cups water
      1½ cups sugar
      4 heaping tablespoons cornstarch

In an 8- or 10-inch Dutch oven, cook until thick. Add 1 teaspoon almond or lemon extract. Cool slightly. Have a single pie crust molded and baked. Put sliced fresh peaches in the shell and pour the cooked mixture over the top. If you bake the shell directly in a 12-inch Dutch oven, just double the ingredients for the filling. Top with whipped cream. Makes 8-12 servings.

Royalty Raspberry Sour Cream Pie

Rosemary Parkinson and Peggy Roskelly

1 baked pie shell in a 12-inch Dutch oven

Sour Cream Filling

1½ cups sugar
6 tablespoons cornstarch
2 teaspoons grated lemon rind
¼ cup lemon juice

1 cup cultured sour cream
⅓ cup butter
5 egg yolks slightly beaten
2 cups milk

Raspberry Glaze

3 tablespoons cornstarch
1 cup sugar
pinch of salt

⅛ teaspoon vanilla
½ cup water
4 dry pints of raspberries

To make filling:

Combine sugar, cornstarch, lemon rind, juice, egg yolks, and milk in a Dutch oven or heavy saucepan. Cook over medium heat until thick. Stir in butter and cool mixture to room temperature. Stir in the sour cream and pour filling into the cooled pie shell. Cover with the glaze.

To make glaze:

Mix 2 pints berries and water and heat to release juice. Strain. Mix sugar, cornstarch and salt and add the strained juice. Cook over medium heat until thick. Cool. When cool, add fresh berries and spoon over the top of the pie. Makes 8-12 servings.

Flaky Pie Dough

½ cup ice water plus a squeeze of lemon
1 egg, beaten
1¾ cups shortening
4 cups flour, sifted, then measured
1 teaspoon salt

Combine the shortening, flour and salt. Work these ingredients together with two forks, a pastry blender, or your hands, until they are the size of large peas. Combine the water mixture and beaten egg and pour into the shortening mixture a little at a time and work until the dough is moist. Extreme care should be taken not to overwork the dough. Divide the dough into half. Use these portions as two bottom crusts or a top and a bottom crust for a 12-inch Dutch oven. Makes 2 12-inch crusts.

Lemon Cloud Pie

1 pie shell baked in a 12-inch Dutch oven
12 eggs
2 cups sugar
7 tablespoons cornstarch
2½ cups boiling water
12 tablespoons sugar
dash of salt
juice and rind of 4 large or 6 small lemons

Squeeze the lemons and grate the yellow part of the rind. In a 10- or 12-inch Dutch oven, combine the 2 cups of sugar, 7 tablespoons of cornstarch and the lemon rind. When mixed, add the lemon juice a little at a time. Separate the eggs, putting the yolks in the sugar mixture and reserving the whites for the meringue. Stir the sugar-yolk mixture until there are no more lumps. *Slowly* add the 2½ cups boiling water. Heat over a medium-hot fire until the filling is transparent. Set aside to cool.

Mix egg whites and salt. Whip until mixture starts to thicken.

Gradually add the 12 tablespoons sugar, beating well after each addition, until peaks form.

Fold ¼ of meringue into filling and pour into prepared shell. Place remaining meringue on top of filling, sealing edges to crust. Bake for 12-15 minutes with top heat or until golden brown. Makes 8-12 servings.

Delicious Apple Pie

10 large golden delicious or granny smith apples
1 cup white sugar
⅔ cup brown sugar
3 heaping tablespoons flour
1 tablespoon cinnamon
½ teaspoon nutmeg
½ teaspoon salt
8 ounces cream cheese, softened
1 recipe Flaky Pie Dough (page 98)

Prepare the pie dough as described on page 98. Use half of the dough to form the bottom crust and reserve the other half for the top crust.

Peel and core the apples into a large bowl. Add the remaining ingredients except the cream cheese. Stir gently until the apples are covered with the sugar cinnamon mixture. Add the cream cheese and stir gently until the cream cheese is incorporated.

Pour into the pie shell and place the top crust. Crimp the edges and make steam vents in the top crust. Bake over a 350° fire for two to three hours or until the crust is well browned and the filling is bubly. Serves 8-12 hungry people.

Raspberry and Cream Cheese Pie

2 8-ounce pkgs. cream cheese, room temperature
2 cups sugar
3 tablespoons cornstarch
2 dry quarts red raspberries
1 recipe Flaky Pie Dough (page 98)

Prepare the pie dough as described on page 98. Use half of the dough to form the bottom crust and reserve the other half for the top crust.

If the raspberries are dirty or dusty, wash gently under cold water and then blot dry. If raspberries are not dirty do not wash them. Combine the cream cheese, sugar and cornstarch in a mixing bowl and stir until the mixture is smooth. Add the dry raspberries and stir gently. Spoon the filling into the prepared pie shell and place the top crust. Crimp the edges and make steam vents in the top crust. Bake over a 350° fire for one to one-and-a-half hours or until the crust is well browned and the filling is bubbly.
Serves 8-12 hungry people.

Red Raspberry Pie

2 dry quarts of red raspberries
2 cups sugar
5 tablespoons cornstarch
2 tablespoons grated orange rind
1 recipe Flaky Pie Dough (page 98)

Prepare the pie dough as described on page 98. Use half of the dough to form the bottom crust and reserve the other half for the top crust.

If the raspberries are dirty or dusty, wash gently under cold water, then blot dry. If raspberries are not dirty do not wash them. Stir the berries, sugar, cornstarch and orange rind together in a bowl. Spoon the filling into the prepared pie shell and place the top crust. Crimp the edges and make steam vents in the top crust. Bake over a 350° fire for one to one-and-a-half hours or until the crust is well browned and the filling is bubbly.

Chapter 15

Competition Cooking

This chapter will present a few ideas of how you can be better prepared for a competition. I will describe some of the things that happen at a cook-off and what most judges look for.

One of the first things you need to do as a potential contestant in any cook-off is to understand your motivation. Why do you want to cook in the competition? There are many reasons for cooking in a competition and I don't feel any of the reasons are bad reasons. If you know why you are at a cook-off, you will know how serious to get about the competition. Let me name just three reasons that come to me right off the top of my head.

1. Some people love the glory and fame of winning. They only go to the big competitions with the big prizes. There is nothing wrong with that. If winning is your motivation you will look at competitions differently than some of the other contestants.

2. Another group of contestants is the group of people who go to watch others and how they make their entries. These people go to the competitions to learn another trick or two from the pros. They are not as concerned with winning the money as with learning the techniques. This type of contestant in a competition is very rare. Most people who only want to learn the technique will come and observe from the sidelines only. If you are a sideline note taker, may I encourage you to break down and enter a competition. You will learn more from the "hands on" experience of

being in a competition than you will ever pick up from the sidelines. This is really how I got my start. I didn't have any great wins my first year in competition but I sure learned a lot more talking to the other contestants than anyone could ever learn on the sidelines.

3. A third group of people are those who just come to the cook-offs because they have a lot of friends who enter every year and they meet a lot of new friends each year at the cook-offs. Don't get me wrong, these cooks are very good cooks. They usually place each year they compete. But the competition is not their main reason for being there. Many people claim that Dutch oven cooks are among the most friendly folks in the world. I tend to agree with that thought. Once you have been around Dutch oven cooks you will notice that there is a big difference from other cooks.

Read the Rules

Be sure to read the rules BEFORE you get to the competition. As strange as it may sound, each competition I have been in will invariably get at least one person that will not have read the rules. Most of the time these people just assume the rules will be the same as they were the year before. This is generally not true. Most Dutch oven cook-offs are new enough that they have not had years to perfect the system and work out all the bugs. Therefore, the rules usually do change from year to year. Most of the time the rule changes may not be large but they could be dangerous if you are not aware of them. For example, one year at the World's Championship Dutch Oven Cook Off they allowed the food to be presented to the judges in anything from the cast iron Dutch oven to fancy china and crystal. That was when the cook-off committee decided the competitions were going in the wrong direction. People were spending more time on garnishing and putting the food into fancy dishes than cooking good Dutch oven food. The next year there was a new rule stating that all food must be presented to the judge in the Dutch oven or on the lid. If you had not read the rules before coming you may have brought all your fancy china and not been able to use it. Another example of the necessity of reading the rules would be if the rules spell out a particular way you need to write a recipe card for your entry. If you didn't read the rules you may be forced to rewrite your recipe, leaving less time to prepare your entry. This could be fatal. Please remember to read the rules!

Judges

In a Dutch oven competition you will generally find two types of judges. These judges are known as field judges and food judges. In smaller competitions they may only have one judge but that person will still be looking for the same things that the two judges would be in a large competition. Because the World Championship Dutch Oven Cook Off is the largest Dutch oven competition in the world, I will explain how the judging is done there.

A field judge is responsible for making sure that all contestants come to the competition with clean Dutch ovens. If a Dutch oven has a skiff of old ashes the field judge takes away a point or two for cleanliness. Cleanliness points can also be docked if the contestant doesn't keep his cooking area clean and his hands and utensils washed. The field judge is there to insure that all contestants follow all the rules for preparation such as the number of ovens you can use or the types of cooking aids you can use in the Dutch oven. Some years you are able to use a saucepan inside your Dutch oven and other years you are not. One year contestants were not even allowed to use tin foil. If there are any infractions of the rules the field judge will dock the contestant the appropriate amount of points. These demerits are predetermined before the competition ever starts. Another important function of the field judge is to judge the cook's cooking ability in a Dutch oven. If a person bakes a beautiful peach pie in a pie pan inside the Dutch oven and another contestant also cooks a peach pie but cooks it directly in the Dutch oven, the field judge should take a few "cooking technique points" away from the contestant that baked the pie in the pie pan. The pie may be just as good or maybe even better. But judging the contestant on technique, the contestant that baked the pie directly in the Dutch oven should get more points because it is harder to do.

Last of all, the field judge is usually the one who calls the contestants to the judging table to have their entry judged by the food judge or judges. The field judge is responsible to tell the contestant how much time is left until each contestant will be judged and also makes sure that all the food that was prepared makes it up to the judging table. In this cook off there is no hiding the burned rolls!

The food judges will look at the entry when it is brought to the judging table. They judge on appearance, taste, texture, doneness, flakiness, etc. These are the judges you need to impress with your garnishes and decorating ability. Some competitions may let you serve your meal any way you like. Others, including the World Championship Dutch Oven Cook Off, will require the entry to be presented in the Dutch oven or on the lid. Remember, you must read the rules to find out how your entry is to be presented to the judges before you get to the competition.

Choosing a Winning Recipe

I have often had people ask me what recipe I think will win the competition for them. I honestly have to tell these people that I have no idea. Each judge looks for different things and has, I'm sorry to say, his own bias. Each judge also has a different level of experience in food judging. Therefore, it is impossible to predict what will be the winning dish. I always say to choose a recipe that shows off your abilities. But don't make it so hard that you push yourself out of the competition. A simple recipe done well will always score higher than a recipe that is hard and flops. Remember that a competition is to assess your abilities so if you can make it from scratch — do it. Anyone can make a cake mix. But it takes a little expertise to bake a sourdough cake. Anyone can cook a roast but it takes a good cook to make a tender morsel out of a tough cut of beef. A good judge will look for these things.

Garnishing

After you have found the perfect recipe for the competition, a very important thing is to garnish it in a way to make it pleasing to the eye as well as to the taste. A little sprig of parsley or a slight dusting of powdered sugar may make the whole difference.

Garnishing — a treat for the eyes.

There are numerous books you can find in your local library with good garnishing ideas. I like to also look through the cookbook section of book stores and see how the food is displayed in the pictures. Your own creativity can also be used. Be careful, however, that your garnish complements the entry, not overpowers it. One year on Dessert Night of the World Championship Dutch Oven Cook Off I cooked a recipe called Festival Fudge. It is a no-fail creamy fudge made with marshmallow and chocolate pieces. When it was set up I cut it into squares and stacked them neatly on my Dutch oven lid. To add a little color I garnished it with parsley. I look back now and wonder how I could ever have used such a mismatched garnish. I guess I was just caught up in the competition and was only looking at the color of the brown and green together.

After the competition one of the judges came up to me and said the fudge was wonderful but I should consider a nice white doily or a sprinkling of powdered sugar, mint leaves or even a maraschino cherry for the garnish but NOT PARSLEY! The point was well taken and now my wife loves to tell the story to all our friends even though we did place third with the fudge.

Schedule

Your schedule in a competition is all important. If your dish is ready 10 minutes before judging time and gets cold you will be docked. If it is only 5 minutes late you may be disqualified for not being ready. Remember unforeseen difficulties may come up that you will need to deal with. For example, if the wind comes up and you are not prepared with a windbreak, you need to be aware that your coals will burn hotter, more uneven and quicker than in calm conditions. You would need to know that you must check and rotate your ovens more frequently to ensure no scorched spot. If possible, look over the location of the cook off before it begins so you will know what type of a surface you will be cooking on. If you are cooking on sand you will need more heat and cooking time than if you are cooking on asphalt or cement. If you are going to cook in a lot of competitions I would suggest you buy or make a portable cooking table to cook on. Most competitions will allow them and then you don't have to guess what the cooking surface will be like at each competition.

On the day of the competition, arrive as early as you can so you will be as relaxed as possible. Practice the dish as many times as possible so you will feel in control and know what to do and when to do it. It is a lot easier to handle a rough situation in your backyard and work it out than to have a judge staring at you to see how you will deal with it.

No one has all the answers of how to win the prize money but I hope that some of the information in this chapter will help you in your pursuit. Good luck! I hope you have as much fun at competitions as I do!

Chapter 16

Large Group Cooking and Catering

When people heard I had won a division in the World's Championship Dutch Oven Cook-off in Logan, Utah, I started getting calls to cook for very large groups. At first I was very nervous about this because I had no experience in this field. But then I realized I didn't have any experience when I entered the cook-off either. I started telling people I would do it, and once again I started learning very quickly.

The most important thing I learned was that you need to be *very organized* if you want everything to turn out well. I sit down and make two lists. First, a list of all the tools and equipment I will need and the second, a grocery list. After you have catered one or two parties, this part is really easy because you just have to look at your previous lists. To help you make your own list, I will give you a list of tools I use for large-group cooking at the end of this chapter.

After I decide what will be cooked, I then go back to my basic tool list and add any specialty tools needed. The grocery list is then easy to come up with from your menu. Check the items needed against the items you already have on hand so you won't end up over-buying.

The hardest part of catering is to plan when and how to prepare the meal. I say this is the hard part because one month ahead of the dinner, you have no idea of what the weather conditions will be or what personal crises you will run into as you are preparing the meal. In order to accommodate for this,

I always try to give myself plenty of extra time. Prepare as much as you can before the day of the party. Also, go to the site where the meal will be prepared and see if there will be any special needs for the party concerning the site. Make sure there is adequate space in the areas in which you will cook, serve, eat and clean-up.

Another key point is to try to "over plan" the party. If you over plan, it is less likely that you forget something. Acquire all food and supplies at least the day before. Non-perishables can even be purchased the week before to help eliminate some of the stress. Try to get a good night's sleep the night before the party. Cooking in twenty Dutch ovens can be tiring. And be sure to have enough help when you start cooking and getting ready for the party. If there is anything you can do ahead of time, do it!

Tools and Supplies Needed

Hot water

Apron

Tongs (fire)

Tongs (food)

Nets to cover food (flies)

Needle and thread

Matches

Charcoal lighters

Dutch oven tools

Oil

Dish towels

Coolers

Plastic garbage bags

Spices

Paper and pencils

Spoons

Aspirin

Marble slab

Recipes

Measuring cups

Dutch ovens

Cold water

Cutting board

Baster

Tables

Chairs

Knives

Charcoal

Lighter fluid

Whisk broom

Paper towels

Bowls

Tablecloths

Salt and pepper

Dish soap (for knives, etc.)

Eggbeaters

Serving utensils

Rolling pin

Grater

Cooling racks

Hot pads

Chapter 17

Dutch Ovens in Food Storage Programs

A Dutch oven is just the food storage item you need to be prepared for a major or minor disaster in your area. I have heard it said that anything can be cooked in a Dutch oven that you can cook in a regular oven. With a little imagination and a lot of practice, this can be absolutely true. You don't need any special tools to add to your emergency supplies other than the regular tools you already use for Dutch oven cooking. However, you do need to store a supply of fuel to cook on. You can use a gas barbecue grill, bags of charcoal, or even wood.

If you elect to store charcoal briquettes, store them in a dry place and rotate them every year so they will remain lightable. If your area is prone to flooding don't store them in the basement. Store them in a place they will be easy to get to and be sure to store enough to meet the needs of your family. When you are cooking a whole meal you can really go through quite a few briquettes.

If you are planning to use your gas barbecue grill in case of an emergency, be sure to have the propane or gas tank filled all the time and possibly have a reserve tank on hand. You may also want to check to make sure your Dutch ovens will fit inside your barbecue to be sure you'll be able to use your barbecue grill. If your grill is too small you will have to use another heat source.

Wood as a heat source would be my last choice for a food storage item. Wood fires smoke a lot and it takes a lot of wood to get the needed coals to cook on. The woodpile where the wood is stored is also an inconvenience and possibly an eyesore if your yard area is small. However, though wood may be a little less convenient it still works very well in a food storage program. Some people already have woodpiles for fireplaces or wood-burning stoves. For them, wood in their food storage program would be a natural.

No matter what type of heat source you use in your food storage program you ought to practice using it before you have an emergency. If you don't, you may be very hungry before you get your first meal made. Remember that each of the heat sources heat and cook differently than the others.

Along with storing briquettes, propane, or wood for your heat source, don't forget to have extra oil and paper towels or rags to keep your ovens clean. If your ovens are not cleaned the residue in them can mold or rust. Both these conditions can ruin your seasoning and pit the inside surface of your oven. This can make your ovens still harder to clean, and if severely pitted, can cause weak spots or hot spots in the cast iron.

Only store things in your emergency food storage supply your family will eat. Some people store a lot of canned soups, rice, beans and wheat. With these simple staples you can make a wide variety of meals. My family really likes homemade scones and rice with a sauce made from cream of chicken soup over it. If you can, try to use some of the items from your food storage once a week or so. This will help alleviate the problem of spoilage of food-storage items. Your family will also be used to eating the items in your food storage so eating it in an emergency situation wouldn't be a great shock to anyone's system.